WILLIAM ARRUDA

DIGITAL YOU

Real Personal Branding in the Virtual Age

PRESS

ATD Press is an internationally renowned source of insightful and practical information on talent development, training, and professional development.

ATD Press
1640 King Street
Alexandria, VA 22314 USA

Ordering information: Books published by ATD Press can be purchased by visiting ATD's website at www.td.org/books or by calling 800.628.2783 or 703.683.8100.

Library of Congress Control Number: 2019945723

ISBN-10: 1-949036-75-8
ISBN-13: 9781949036756
e-ISBN: 9781949036763

ATD Press Editorial Staff
Director: Sarah Halgas
Manager: Melissa Jones
Community of Practice Manager, Career Development: Lisa Spinelli
Developmental Editor: Kathryn Stafford
Production Editor: Hannah Sternberg
Text and Cover Design: Michelle Jose

Printed by Versa Press, East Peoria, IL

Contents

Introduction

Personal Branding Is Dead

That headline might seem heretical—not to mention self-defeating—coming from me, a pioneer in the field of personal branding.

But it's true.

At least, it's true that the concept of personal branding as we once defined it has no more life in it. It's no longer relevant. It's nothing more than a relic.

RIP old personal branding.

We didn't know it then, but analog personal branding was a mere prototype for the glorious, global, digital branding machine that today's workforce is learning to operate.

But before we lay to rest the personal branding of yesterday, let's take a trip down memory lane (at warp speed).

The idea of personal branding was not an instant hit. Take it from me. I was there at the beginning. Personal branding simmered for many years and was predicted to be little more than a passing fad. When Tom Peters coined the term back in 1997, few people knew what it meant, and even fewer were interested in building their brand.

The acceptance of personal branding was slow because the circumstances that require it hadn't fully formed. Just eight years after Tom Peters's prophetic article, "The Brand Called You," was published, the magazine that featured it on its cover—*Fast Company*—decided that they had made a mistake. They declared personal branding dead before any life was ever breathed into it (Lidsky 2005). And it's true, in 2005 professionals weren't feeling stressed about their long-term career prospects and most people still worked alongside their colleagues in corporate towers or suburban office parks. The Internet was in its infancy. And the product that changed how we communicate, the iPhone, didn't make its debut until 2007. It wasn't until 2014 that the Internet was accessible in 80 percent of U.S. homes, according to the U.S. Census Bureau.

But rapid changes in the global marketplace, combined with multiple, serious downturns in the economy, led career-minded professionals to start taking notice of the potential for personal branding to serve as a career management strategy. From there, even if they didn't know exactly what it is, executives realized that having a brand is an essential career asset that can help them reach their goals. And companies got in on the act, too. Most major corporations have adopted personal branding programs into their talent development initiatives. My company alone supports 20 percent of the Fortune 100 and dozens of global brands, associations, and institutions.

Ironically, now that personal branding has made it to the big league, there's talk that the personal branding revolution is over. I hear about it all the time—from the press and career coaches to HR executives. It's true that pseudo-branding has lost its cachet, but the new era of digital personal branding is not only thriving but vital to success.

Let me set the record straight by describing three reasons why naysayers have muddled the truth about the personal branding revolution, which I can assure you is alive and well.

1. **Message overload.** You're inundated with messages all day long: ads, emails, app alerts, texts, tweets. It's easy to think that personal branding is next to impossible now that the roar of the crowd is almost deafening. But silence is not the answer. Quite the opposite. Today's tools for digital personal branding provide clever ways to differentiate yourself, presenting your valuable message to the right people at the right time. The same tools that caused Information

Age overload can help you rise above the roar and get noticed when you use them effectively.

2. **Misunderstanding.** Many people confound personal branding with self-promotion, bragging, or manufactured pristine personas created by a self-centered generation. The term *personal branding* has become hijacked by those who associate it with mindless, endless online chatter and the grandiose desire to be visible, known, and popular. Equating personal branding with social media excess has distorted the true value of personal branding. Personal branding is not a TMZ story about the Kardashians. And it's certainly not about visibility for the sake of being visible. In fact, personal branding is not about you. It's about how you deliver value to others.

3. **Myopia.** Ironically, the third reason some people think personal branding is dead is related to the rise of virtual employees. Companies, once reluctant to let their people work from home for fear that they would goof off, are now becoming proponents of remote work. They are encouraging their employees to keep away from the office; in a 2015 Gallup study, the number of American workers who have telecommuted climbed to 37 percent. The cost savings to companies are just too big to ignore. But as work becomes more virtual, employees often have the erroneous belief that they're free from having to brand themselves because their work will speak for itself. Without the distraction of face-to-face chats at the coffee station, the quality of the work takes center stage, right? Nothing could be further from the truth. We all know the old adage: out of sight, out of mind. Virtual employees have to work harder to be relevant and remain top-of-mind. They must use new ways to visibly demonstrate their value. Being virtual can mean being invisible, and digital personal branding is the solution.

Personal branding has taken on a completely new life since the days when it was only being used by senior execs in large corporations. Today, college students are using it to stand out so they can land internships. Some universities have added branding courses to their curriculum. Even high school students are perfecting their LinkedIn profiles to help them secure a spot in the college of their choice.

In my own business, I can see how it has become a thread seamlessly woven into the fabric of career management. In 2018, my company signed on eight new corporate clients for personal branding programs (two of them rank in the top 10 places to work). My company's personal branding certification programs (now delivered by Career Thought Leaders) had near-record attendance, and the number of Google alerts I received on the term *personal branding* increased 30 percent over the past year.

Personal Branding Is Dead.
Long Live Personal Branding.

Let's focus on where personal branding is today, where it's headed, and what you need to be thinking about so you can remain relevant. Let's be clear: Your personal brand is your most valuable career asset when you know how to uncover, express, and nurture it.

Personal Branding Reboot: Nine Key Trends

There are nine business and career trends that are influencing how you need to think about—and strategically manage—your brand. Understanding these trends is critical to your ability to amp up your success and happiness at work.

1. Nexting

Today's youngest workers are more likely to have 15 or more jobs in their lifetime.

Tenure is down.

The time we spend in companies is waning. According to the U.S. Bureau of Labor Statistics, the average worker has held 10 different jobs. Today's youngest workers are more likely to have 15 or more jobs in their lifetimes. That's at least 50 percent more jobs. According to a study by Nintex, 53 percent of employees don't expect to stay at their companies beyond five years. And Deloitte's 2018 Millennial Survey revealed that Gen Zers expect to stay with their current employer for fewer than two years (Previte 2019). At the same time, the life expectancy of companies is shrinking. The security you feel "working for the man" is probably false security. The new career mantra is "What's next?"

Although successful branding is based in authenticity, an element of aspiration is essential to career success. You need to plan for (and be prepared for) what's next. In the book *Switchers: How Smart Professionals Change Careers and Seize Success,* Dawn Graham points out the importance of ensuring your brand is aligned with the growing professional network you seek to influence.

"Today's job market is shifting so quickly that career changes, hybrid roles, and budding industries are becoming the new normal," she told me by email, "so it's important that everyone understand how to rebrand for a career transition. Professionals often have a wealth of transferable skills and experiences that make them both qualified, as well as unique, for open positions, but my mantra is 'match first, stand out second.' Too often, job seekers fail to brand to their target audience, relaying impressive achievements that unfortunately aren't relevant to the role. Those achievements will serve you well when you bring them up at the right time—for example, to demonstrate a competitive advantage over the other finalists when you're on the verge of an offer."

What's more, retirement has been completely redefined. We're living longer—giving us an opportunity to write a complete chapter 2 of our careers (or chapter 16 if we think there will be 15 distinct roles in our "official" career). The idea of retirement has all but disappeared. Navigating this major career milestone requires preparation—a longer-term mindset for your career planning.

2. Flextrapreneurship

"We're definitely seeing a trend where professionals want more control over when, where, and how they work, and they're turning to remote work to get it."
—Brie Reynolds, Senior Career Specialist at FlexJobs

Rigidity is gone when it comes to the entrepreneurial–intrapreneurial divide. There is an increasing fluidity between working for a company and working for *your* company. Countless online communities are being built to support this paradigm. Remote.com, for example, with more than 2 million members, brings together people who are working remotely for a company with entrepreneurs and solopreneuers.

Moreover, companies are seeking the entrepreneurial mindset when hiring talent. In her SlideShare "Five Ways to Get Your Team Thinking Like Entrepreneurs," Sophia Ellis, head of content at the productivity app Hibox, writes, "The companies with the most entrepreneurial-thinking team members are going to be the ones that surpass all others despite how big they are, where they started, and how they started to provide just that. An entrepreneurial mindset is something that must be both hired in and fostered in companies of any size to guarantee success in the new business landscape."

3. Digital First

"11 percent of Gen Zers google themselves every day."
—Bank of America

You may not need to google yourself every day, but you do need to know what's out there and proactively manage how you show up online. Like it or not, your Google results are quickly becoming your first impression. When people want to learn about you, they'll open up a browser, enter your name, and see what comes up. I call it *he-surfing* or *she-surfing*, and it's a phenomenon that's here to stay. In his eye-opening book, *Ctrl Alt Delete,* digital media expert Mitch Joel speaks of a digital-first posture. He acknowledges that the web is often the first place we go when we want to learn about something—or someone. The implications of this phenomenon are huge when it comes to career success. Eighty percent of employers admit to googling potential employees before they hire them.

We live in a relationship economy, where influencing others is essential. If your initial impression is anemic or inauthentic, you're squandering opportunities and will be left behind. We'll talk more about the connection between virtual branding, your career success, and the three cognitive biases that come into play in chapter 4.

4. Brandscaping

More than 100,000 articles are posted on LinkedIn each week,
and 576,000 hours of video are uploaded to YouTube every day.

It's a noisy world. To be heard in this world requires steadfast clarity and focus. You'll get lost in the clamor if your message isn't clear, consistent, and constant (the three Cs of strong brands, which we'll talk about later in the book). Brandscaping is all about trimming the extraneous stuff that distracts, detracts, or disorients so your image comes across pristine and potent.

You need to build your brand around something—not a hundred things. That's way too complicated for people to figure out. It's cacophonous. But when you are singing the same note all the time, you can be recognized and remembered. Just as Volvo is known for safety and Apple is synonymous with innovation, you must distill your brand into that nugget of value that you want people to hear from you, repeated often, like a refrain. In our over-stimulated 24/7 world of nonstop communications, people just don't have the time or inclination to try to figure you out. Unless you're working for a startup or you're a one-person show, being a jack-of-all-trades will work against you. Focus needs to be your mantra.

5. Treadmill Learning

"We accept the fact that learning is a lifelong process of keeping abreast of change. And the most pressing task is to teach people how to learn."
—Peter Drucker

You can't stand still on a treadmill that's in motion. If you don't keep moving forward, you'll fall off the back and be left behind. The same is true of learning in the new world of work. If you aren't actively learning every day, you'll quickly lose your relevance and gain the reputation of being a reluctant, reticent relic. In addition, your company is no longer responsible for telling you what to learn or how to grow professionally. But compared to Peter Drucker's era, we have learned so much about how to learn. It's never been so easy to expand your horizons using methods that suit your budget, your learning style, and your calendar.

Most of the responsibility—and opportunity—for learning has been switched to you. And that's great news! According to Kelly Palmer in her book, *The Expertise Economy: How the Smartest Companies Use Learning to Engage, Compete, and Succeed,* "The one-size-fits-all mentality of corporate education is no longer relevant. Learning needs to be customized for each individual based on their skill and knowledge gaps, personal and professional goals, and specific interests." That puts the onus on you to determine what to learn and how to obtain your learning. Palmer adds, "One of the main goals of personalized learning is ultimately to combine the best of what the ecosystem has to offer. It's not an either/or proposition, but rather aims to unite the best features of learner motivation, technology, and online learning supported by teacher and peer expertise."

With that in mind, I've created this book to give you personalized learning opportunities at every turn. (Yes, reading this book counts as a giant leap in your learning.)

6. Digital Advocacy

Employees have on average 10 times more social connections than a brand does, and brand messages reached 561 percent further when shared by employees vs. the same messages shared via official brand social channels. Brand messages are reshared 24 times more frequently when distributed by employees vs. the brand (Burke 2017).

We're witnessing one of the greatest contradictions in business history. On one hand, the 30-year, lifelong career with the same company is gone, and you're expected to operate as more of a free agent even when you're "working for the man." Yet company loyalty is highly valued. How can that be? The answer is that "company loyalty" has taken a new form.

In the past, your career success was related to focusing on your role, function, and department. Today, success requires that you be a company brand ambassador and megaphone, even if you're not going to stay with that company for more than a few years. Company communications used to be a solo act. The CEO, via the communications department, would decide what to say, whom the audience would be, and which medium would be used. Today, corporate messaging comes from a chorus. And nowhere is this more important than online.

Companies need this chorus of messaging because stakeholders crave transparency. It's the collective voice that helps support the corporate mission, and your voice must be a part of that. This not only benefits the company, it also benefits you and your free-agent mindset. When you do commit to interacting with company-produced social content, you move yourself outside the normal hierarchy, learn what's going on in other areas of the company, and expand your visibility with your own online community. Mark Burgess, president of Blue Focus Marketing and co-author of *The Social Employee,* puts it this way: "We live in an era of fake news and a decline in trust that extends to our institutions, politicians, and brands. In this new atmosphere, brands that are seen as self-serving and focused on profits at the expense of people and/or the environment are likely to fail. The new competitive advantage is trust, and engaged, empowered social employees are the fuel that powers purpose-driven brands."

7. Distance Branding

Seventy percent of Millennials have left or considered leaving a job because it lacked flexible work options, while only about half of older workers report the same (Howington 2018). By 2020, almost half of the workforce will be made up of Millennials (Weber 2013).

Proximity is down. More and more, people are working some or all of the time remotely. "Work Anywhere Anytime" is the new career chant. Companies are taking advantage of the communications tools that allow for virtual employees to engage and interact. Some companies track badge swipes at their offices, and if you don't make the threshold of the minimum number of office visits each month, you no longer have the right to an office—or even a hot desk. Organizations know that when people work from home, they save the company expensive real-estate costs. They also understand that employees are demanding flexibility when it comes to work.

While this new "work anywhere" model is making companies more financially competitive and more attractive to the latest generation of workers, it comes with new challenges: Employees feel less connected to what's going on. A 2018 report from WorkplaceTrends.com finds that for employees who depend on email to communicate with teammates, more than 40 percent said they feel lonely always or very often, are not engaged, and have a high need for social connection. The study also found that a third of employees globally work remotely always or very often, and two-thirds of them aren't engaged. Only 5 percent of remote workers always or very often see themselves working at their company for their entire career, compared with 28 percent who never work remotely.

What does this mean for you? The hurdles for personal branding can be high. You'll need to become more deliberate and focused on branding, which will require more effort to create familiarity, recognition, and connection with colleagues. You can't achieve your goals if you don't build relationships and influence decision makers. These needs are only going to become more pressing. Remote work is here to stay, and it's poised to rocket even higher. Nick Marcario, co-founder and CEO of Remote.com, says, "It's no secret work is changing as the workforce mobilizes. There is an abundance of research and statistics that illustrate how prominent the shift is and how much it's expected to accelerate in the future."

8. Digital Dexterity

"Seventy-six percent of CEOs are concerned about the lack of digital skills within their own workforce—and 23 percent are extremely concerned about the digital skills of their leadership team."
—PwC 21st CEO Survey: Talent

The one skill that's required across industries, functions, and levels is digital dexterity. Companies know that to maintain a competitive advantage, they need a workforce that is digitally enabled and enabling, because the most visible innovations emerge from technology—and from employees who know how to translate high tech into a high-impact experience for customers.

The world's largest professional services firm, PwC, with more than a quarter million employees and partners, even created a new executive role—chief digital officer—to ensure all employees have the digital skills necessary to innovate internally and impress their clients externally. They tapped a senior partner, Joe Atkinson, to lead the initiative. He told me: "My role is to be 'a constructive disrupter.' My mission is to enhance digital fitness throughout the organization and put in place the learning and technology necessary to get the entire organization comfortable with the language and concepts that are driving digital innovation."

That means whether you're working in marketing, accounts payable, or legal, you need to bulk up your digital muscle, knowing which developments—from artificial intelligence and robotics to data analytics and new social media platforms—can become valuable assets for your team.

9. YOUcasting

*"Globally, Internet video traffic will grow four-fold from 2017 to 2022,
a compound annual growth rate of 33 percent" (Cisco).*

I used to say that video is the future of personal branding. Well, the future has arrived! Video allows you to deliver a complete communication and connect more deeply and emotionally with those you seek to influence. Video is becoming a significant communications tool and will ultimately replace email and texting as a more powerful and valuable medium. YouTube is already the second-largest search engine after Google, according to Search Engine Journal (2018).

According to experiments done by psychologist Albert Mehrabian, words account for only 7 percent of whether a communicator is likable, and the rest is determined by tone of voice, intonation, and body language. See why video is such a powerful tool for personal branding? Virtually all the trends we have discussed so far are creating the opportunity for video to take over as our primary communications vehicle. Video skills are just as essential as, if not more than, writing or public speaking. Video conferences will replace teleconferences and vmail will become the new email. Professionals who get comfortable with this medium will remain relevant and compelling. Those who stick with the 26 letters of the alphabet will be left behind.

Live Between the Hyphens

You might feel a little daunted right now. How can you become a remote-but-visible, high-tech, high-touch, remote-yet-embedded, independent-but-loyal, video-producing, content-generating brand ambassador for yourself? The key word is *you*. Digital or not, successful branding is always rooted in authenticity, and effective messaging is rooted in simplicity. Even if you have never considered that you have a brand, your current LinkedIn profile is nearly blank, or you have relied on your organization to manage your career, I'll share with you everything you need to know and do so you can take advantage of this new digital branding phenomenon. My approach will help you find your true self between those hyphens, unearthing the traits that help you thrive and then showcasing them using methods that are efficient and effective. What does it take to tap the power of personal branding in the digital age? Nothing less than a total mindset reset.

About This Book

In *Digital You*, I'll teach you how to master the new rules and tools for staying relevant, visible, and valuable in a world of work that is continually being reinvented. It's time to stop worrying about career extinction and start crafting a brand of distinction. This is true regardless of who you are or where you are in your career. Whether you're new to the work world, mid-career, or greatly experienced; whether you're in career transition, just hired, a consultant looking to branch out, an entrepreneur trying to break in, or any combination thereof, this book is for you.

A few years ago, I was feeling untethered (read: lonely) and wanted to connect to a community—my community. That's the challenge with being a public speaker and the entrepreneur of a completely virtual organization. Since most of my work is speaking, I decided to go to the annual National Speakers Association event in Philly (just a quick train ride from NYC) to connect with other speakers in person. My expectations were high. I thought I was going to fit right in with a community of like-minded professional speakers, but in fact it was quite the opposite. I found that the speakers were impressive, inspiring, and engaging, but what the conference lacked for me was authenticity, application, and action.

I realized that my brand differentiation as a speaker is that I don't try to comply with the "standard rules of public speaking." I don't rehearse my presentations a thousand times until every movement, gesture, and inflection is memorized. I'm not an actor. I've never delivered the same keynote the same way twice. And the inspirational part of public speaking is just that for me—part of the experience. The other part—and my favorite part—is in the action. I don't just want to fuel people up and have the fuel leak out of the tank over time. I want to compel them to combust that fuel—taking action so they can turn that fuel into focus, and then turn focus into future success.

I take the same approach in my role of author. I don't want you to just learn some interesting things about digital branding. I did not set out to write a book about digital branding theory. I want you to apply what you learn, taking action and moving your career forward while amping up the joy factor at work.

To that end, this book is designed to be read—and acted upon—serially. It follows a logical order that will help you get to the top of your career the way you would ascend a staircase—one step at a time. Even if you feel you have a good understanding of your brand, don't skip part 1. It will help you clarify and refine your thinking before you move into digital branding—making your social branding actions that much more potent. I've divided the book into four parts, reflecting the personal digital journey I'm asking you to take—and I'll be along every step of the way.

In Part 1: Real You, I introduce personal branding and invite you to discover where your unique self fits. I help you to define yourself and uncover your brand in chapter 1, and better understand the perceptions others have of you and why those are important in chapter 2, so that you're ready to define the authentic story you want to tell (chapter 3).

In Part 2: Virtual You, I invite you to think about your digital impression. In chapter 4, I help you to understand how the digital-first phenomenon can work for you. In chapter 5, I share how to translate the real you for a digital audience, and in chapter 6, I show how you can expand that digital brand you've created.

In Part 3: Visual You, I show you how you to build on and develop your brand to become a multimedia standout. In chapter 7, I help you see the power of pictures, both still and moving, to carry your digital message. Then, you'll learn how to build your personal brand identity system in chapter 8. In chapter 9, I'll share my favorite video tips to engage and connect, and explain why I'm video's biggest fan and why you should be too.

In Part 4: Social You, I ask you to consider the heights you can reach through digital brand development, your network, and thought leadership. In chapter 10, I help you assess your current networks, both online and off, to build your social network and nurture relationships. In chapter 11, you'll learn how to update, curate, and create content related to your expertise to express your thought leadership and promote others. Finally, in chapter 12, I show you how you can truly enlarge your role to your wider community, becoming a digital advocate.

To fulfill my role of CEO (chief encouragement officer) and action-inspiring branding consultant, I have filled the book with practical opportunities to absorb and apply the content:

 MINDSET RESET

These are important mental shifts you must make to be relevant today and to benefit from all the digital branding revolution has to offer.

 PONDER THIS

These are powerful questions that can help you clarify who you are and what's important. Don't gloss over these questions, especially those where the answer doesn't come to mind quickly.

🔒 BRAND HACK

These are a simple (often uncommon) actions you can take immediately (what I call a super special secret tip) that will have a big impact on your branding with relatively little effort.

✔ DO THIS, ✘ NOT THAT

These are guideposts to direct you to the most productive path and help you avoid pitfalls, time wasters, and trite advice that could actually diminish your brand.

📶 REMOTE CONTROL

This advice is specifically designed for those of you who are working remotely part or all of the time, to help you control your brand despite the distance. Distance branding (trend number 7) is real and will affect every professional now and in the future.

💡 FUN FACT

These are interesting and often surprising statistics that help reinforce a key message or lesson.

👤 BRANDI BRAINSTORMS

To show you how the branding process builds, I'll share some branding elements from a fictional person throughout the book. Brandi is the wildly successful personal brander I created, not in a test tube but on the pages of this book. Her traits are the hybrid of two equally accomplished clients with whom I have worked.

So follow along, taking action as you navigate the chapters, and as my CareerBlast.TV co-founder, Ora Shtull, and I always say, *have a blast!*

Part 1
Real You

*"We are at our most productive and creative when we are happy
and being ourselves at work."*
—Richard Branson

CHAPTER 1

Uncover Your Brand

Who Are You?

Real precedes virtual.

One of the most egregious errors I see in digital branding comes from starting in the middle of the process. Why do I see this error so often? Because so many professionals started building their brand only after the digital tools became available. They began creating visibility without clarity about their message—squandering their efforts and diluting their brand rather than targeting it.

You can't start expressing and expanding your brand in the digital world until you extract your traits. That is, you need to understand exactly what your brand is.

But before we do that, let's take a good look at the cornerstone and define what personal branding is.

When I started my personal branding business about two decades ago, few people had heard of personal branding—and even fewer were interested in building their brand. Today, as Google results reveal, there's lots of talk about personal branding, and virtually every career-minded professional knows its importance. Although awareness is high, misconceptions persist. So let me define personal branding here.

Personal branding is the habit of demonstrating and communicating your unique, valuable traits to communities where you can thrive.

 MINDSET RESET

Personal branding supports not just finding a new job but also finding a job where you'll be happy and appreciated because you and the organization are providing value to each other.

The power of personal branding goes way beyond job search. It's an important part of getting promoted, increasing business success, and enhancing personal fulfillment. Having a strong brand helps you do your job better. Most major corporations realize this and have created programs to help their employees build their brands to increase engagement, performance, and satisfaction.

The Six Laws of Successful Personal Branding

- Everyone has the potential to build a strong and desirable brand.
- Your brand is based in authenticity—who you really are.
- Although based in authenticity, your brand must position you for what's next.
- What others think counts. Your brand is held in the hearts and minds of those around you.
- Personal branding means giving value, not taking. It's not about egotism or chest-pounding.
- Personal branding is not a onetime event. You change, the work landscape changes. Everything around you changes. Your brand must evolve to remain relevant.

Three Stages of Building a Powerful Brand

Relationships are the currency of business.

Now that we understand what branding is, I'd like to introduce you to a model that shows what happens when you build a strong, differentiated, and magnetic brand. I built this model after working with thousands of professionals all over the world and realized that successful brands sit along a continuum (Figure 1-1).

Figure 1-1. The Branding Continuum: 3 Levels of Brand Success

The personal branding process lets you rise from being a mere service provider to becoming a brand in demand. Let's look at the three phases: undifferentiated, distinguished, and demanded.

Undifferentiated

This level of branding is actually not branding at all. It means that what you offer ticks all the boxes—you meet all the eligibility requirements—but you don't deliver anything that makes you unique or memorable. You aren't giving decision makers any reason to go to bat for you. Your relationships with those around you are transactional, not relational, which makes you easier to replace. This puts you in the position of having to actively pursue every opportunity you seek—with little external support, and lots of exertion on your part.

Distinguished

Many of the successful professionals I meet fall into this category. In addition to meeting all the requirements that people seek in you, you offer something valuable that goes beyond the basics. It could be that you deliver more value than the required level, or maybe the way you do what you do is interesting. You're compelling to those who are making decisions about you. Your name comes to mind because you're memorable. This gives you the opportunity to build relationships with people—people who count. When you are Distinguished, you stand out from your peers and start to build a fan club.

Demanded

When you move into the Demanded phase of branding, you move closer to being in a category of one. In addition to offering something beyond what's expected, what you offer clearly comes from you. You also start to build greater visibility and connections with people who matter. You turn your fans into promoters, and they in turn help spread your brand message. That means that your brand takes on a life of its own, which reduces the energy you have to invest in pursuing leads. You start to attract opportunities as opposed to always having to actively seek them. A distinct sign that you've reached this level is when people know who you are, but you have no idea how they know you.

Personal Branding 101: Authenticity

Part of moving through this continuum obviously relies on what you do every day (that is, the experience you create and value you deliver in every interaction you have) and how you do it. But the equally important part has to do with how you talk about it. How you tell your story—and tell the world—who you are and why they should care. I'll help you tell your story in chapter 3.

Now that you can picture the three phases, let's start unearthing the real you.

You can't build your online profile until you understand who you are in the real world. Before you start creating online content, I'm going to make sure you have all the supplies you'll need on your virtual branding journey. I'll share with you personal branding basics—the key things you need to know so you can stand out and fuel your career.

"Be yourself, because everyone else is already taken."
—often attributed to Oscar Wilde

That quip sums up one of the most important tenets of personal branding. All strong brands are based in what's true. Genuine. Real. Disney injects family entertainment into their movies, theme parks, and products— bringing "magic" to everything they do. One-of-a-kind entrepreneur Richard Branson applied his passion for adventure and value of risk-taking to build the iconic Virgin brand. All strong brands are based in authenticity.

If you're like most people, when you think about personal branding, you're thinking about the sexy stuff—building your brand on the web, writing articles, delivering presentations, expanding your network, rivaling Beyoncé's Twitter followers. But if you aren't transparent about what makes you stand out, you'll squander your communications efforts. You must know yourself to grow yourself. That means being introspective. Strong brands know their values and passions, they have documented their goals, and they're fully aware of their superpowers—their signature strengths.

Your brand will topple if it sits on a foundation of inauthenticity. And you'll be worn out, too. Anne Morrow Lindbergh cautioned us when she said, "The most exhausting thing you can be is inauthentic." That's because being someone you're not is hard work. It takes effort to wear a mask. Just ask the stars on Broadway who play a role eight times a week.

If you're disguising the real you, trying to be something you're not, you'll not only be exhausted, you'll be found out.

Girl, You Know It's True

Remember 1990s pop duo Milli Vanilli? Maybe not! Their debut album earned them a Grammy Award for best new artist. Once we learned that they were lip-synching to the music and that they couldn't sing, their Grammy was revoked and we haven't heard from them since.

Because branding is based in authenticity, you need to understand not only who you are but also what makes you compelling to your stakeholders (the people who are making decisions about you). As you think about what makes you you, consider these questions.

 PONDER THIS

What makes you you?
- What are your top values—your operating principles or your nonnegotiables?
- What's your superpower—the thing you do better than anyone else?
- What energizes or ignites you? What are your true passions?
- Why do you do what you do? What's your motivation?

Do you have responses to all these questions? Which ones are the hardest to answer? Give a little extra attention to the ones that make you pause—the ones for which your answer is vague. Those are often the ones that yield the greatest level of learning. If one of these questions has you stumped, take the time to not only find an honest answer but also understand why you struggled to see it.

Personal branding is about being yourself—your best self—without excuses, apologies, or trepidation.

BRAND HACK

Remind yourself to be yourself.

Authenticity is essential, but sometimes it's hard to deliver it consistently. I compiled some brilliant quotes about being yourself.

Here are some of my favorites:

- "You were born an original. Don't die a copy"—John Mason
- "It is the chiefest point of happiness that a man is willing to be what he is."—Desiderius Erasmus
- "Live your truth. Express your love. Share your enthusiasm. Take action towards your dreams. Walk your talk. Dance and sing to your music. Make today worth remembering."—Steve Maraboli
- "To be yourself in a world that is constantly trying to make you something else is the greatest accomplishment."
  —Ralph Waldo Emerson
- "There is just one life for each of us—our own."—Euripides
- "Too many people overvalue what they are not and undervalue what they are."—Malcolm S. Forbes
- "Is life not a hundred times too short for us to stifle ourselves?"
  —Friedrich Nietzsche

You can find my complete collection at www.careerblast.tv/authenticity. Choose the quote that resonates with you and post it somewhere you'll see it as a reminder to be yourself—your best self.

Stand Out

"So you're a little weird? Work it! A little different? Own it!
Better to be a nerd than one of the herd!"
—Mandy Hale, *New York Times* Bestselling Author

One of the most important distinctions in the world of personal branding is the difference between a brand and a commodity. Brands are unique. Desirable. Compelling. They connect with people emotionally and build loyalty. Commodities are interchangeable. If what you offer is the same as others who share your job title, you're a commodity, not a brand. And if you think of yourself as your job title, you're making yourself a commodity—replaceable by anyone else who shares that job title.

When I was living in London managing Lotus branding for IBM EMEA, I came across an amazing dry cleaner. They were amazing because they recognized a trend in professional attire for men—the loss of the necktie. They realized that men were wearing their shirts with the top two buttons open. The challenge with this new more casual style is that shirt collars would inevitably droop by lunchtime, making you look disheveled by the end of the day. In response, this dry cleaner triple starched that part of the shirt—stiffening the shirt to deliver a crisp look that lasted for the entire day. I would go out of my way, walking past numerous other dry cleaners to get to this one, and I would pay double the going rate for my specially starched shirts. They offered something that was not available from anyone else—something beyond what was expected.

That same offer of a unique experience is what you need to strive for as you build your brand. You want people to go out of their way to work with you and for them to pay you what you deserve for the unique value you deliver.

✔ DO THIS,
✘ NOT THAT

Do work your quirks. Understand what makes you stand out and integrate it into all that you do.	Don't think of yourself as your job title. If you do, you're a commodity, not a brand.

If you use your job title to introduce yourself, you're doomed to mediocrity. And you'll forever have to fight to get noticed. Branding is all about the freedom (and the mandate) to differentiate.

Several years ago, I delivered a personal branding keynote in Bucharest, Romania. It was a great gig, and I was blown away by the audience's enthusiasm about brands and branding. The discussion after my presentation went into overtime.

One memorable participant shared this: "The reason we're so excited about brands is that branding gives us choice. Before the wall fell, we didn't have brands of soap; we just had soap. Today, we can choose which soap is right for us. Branding is about a freedom of expression. It's about making our own choice."

Choice Influences Success

Choice influences your ability to reach your goals. A hiring manager chooses you over other qualified candidates. A client chooses you to consult on a project. A director in another part of the organization chooses you to take a leadership role in her department. An employee chooses to apply for a job on your team because of your reputation.

In most instances, decision makers have a choice. You want them to choose you—yet many of us spend a lot of time trying to fit in. We fail to take advantage of our opportunity to be different. The key to successful branding is to stand out.

What Makes You Stand Out?

Let's face it, there are lots of other people with similar qualifications who do what we do. In only rare circumstances does someone fall into a professional category of one (the Queen of England comes to mind). Decision makers have to sort through the masses who seem to offer the same services. When we focus on what we have in common with our colleagues, we become interchangeable. When we focus on our differentiation, we get people excited about us. But effective personal branding requires authentic differentiation. You can't manufacture a set of colorful differences based on what seems to get you noticed or generates media attention. Instead, you have to stand out by what makes you you.

 PONDER THIS

What makes you stand out?

- What do people frequently compliment you on or praise you for?
- What is it that your manager, colleagues, friends, and clients come to you for?
- What adjectives do people consistently use to describe you—perhaps when they're introducing you to others?
- What makes the way you achieve results interesting or unique?
- What's the most unusual or quirkiest thing about you?

Once you understand what separates you from your peers and is relevant and compelling to those who are making decisions about you, think about how you can integrate more of that uniqueness into everything you do every day.

Don't think your brand differentiation needs to be something you acquire, or something directly related to what you do. Sometimes it's just part of who you are. On Hasan Minhaj's Netflix show *Patriot Act,* he is an outsider and insider—Indian, Muslim, American. In the world of American comedians, that's differentiation. Architect Dame Zaha Hadid, who is known for her gorgeous buildings with curvy forms, was the most famous female starchitect. Her gender helped her stand out.

"Work your quirks."

That's the expression Deb Dib, the co-author of my last book, *Ditch. Dare. Do!*, came up with to remind us to exude our differentiation—always.

When you are able to do the job, you're the same as anyone else who meets the requirements. When you add extra value, you start to stand out, and people who want to work with you become your true fans. The ultimate achievement is when you move into phase three—that's when you turn fans into promoters. They become your full-time sales force touting how amazing you are.

Once you're clear about your differentiation, you need to communicate those traits to decision makers so they understand how you will provide value for them. The best way to become known by your differentiation is to integrate it into everything you do and make it visible to those around you. Here's how:

BRAND HACK

Use these three quick steps to brand integration:

1. **Document** the things you do frequently in a normal workday, from communications to the execution of projects.
2. **Think** about how you can integrate your differentiation into those tasks. I share an example in chapter 3 of a creative woman who did just that and garnered the kind of recognition that acts as a rocket booster for your career.
3. **Act.** Bring those quirks to the world stage, weaving them into your daily actions.

This approach will help you attract a well-defined group of decision makers and influencers you are genuinely excited about—and the feeling will be mutual.

Summing Up

In this chapter, I introduced you to the brand continuum and I hope inspired you to take action to become a brand in demand. You put time into some deep reflections so that you know the key elements of your brand—your "why," brand differentiation, superpowers, and other elements that make you irreplaceable. You can articulate your unique promise of value now that you've completed this chapter. But discovering your brand isn't all introspection. In the "Know" phase, you need to learn what others think about you. Since your brand is held in the hearts and minds of those who know you, you must be keenly aware of external perceptions when you're uncovering and defining your brand. In chapter 2, I'm going to help bring the process full circle. You'll validate and refine your self-perceptions by getting feedback from others. Who are the "right" others, you might ask? Well, they're the people who can help you reach your goals. I'll share with you exactly who makes up that community so you can position yourself to influence them.

I find that the overachievers with whom I work are often impatient and eager to take action on building their brand. If that's you, you might be tempted at this point to skip ahead to another chapter, but it won't save you any time in the long run. To build an effective profile that delivers the results you want, you need to complete the Know phase of the personal branding process. It's the only way to make good decisions about what to include, what to exclude, and what to highlight as you express the brand called you. The effort you apply up-front will yield tremendous rewards when it comes time to build your visibility. So relax and enjoy the journey.

CHAPTER 2

Understand Perceptions

What Do People Think About You?

The first step in identifying what people think about you is to determine which people matter. Personal branding is not about being famous. It's about being *selectively* famous. That means you build your brand with only the people who need to know you so you can reach your goals. To this community, you are always visible, available, and valuable. To the rest of the world, you can live in complete obscurity. Isn't it a relief to know that you don't have to be all things to all people? I have a term for this selective audience; I call it your brand community because all the members are providing value to one another.

 MINDSET RESET

Think of your brand community as your 5D team: decision makers, doyens, disciples, defenders, and discoursers. Every effective brand community is made up of people in these categories (Figure 2-1).

Figure 2-1. Your 5D Team

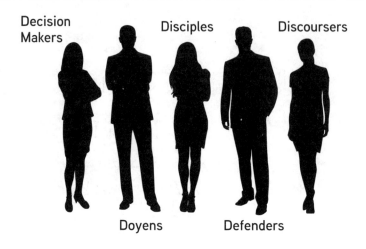

Decision Makers   Disciples   Discoursers

Doyens   Defenders

Decision Makers: These are people who have a major impact on your being able to reach your goals. This category includes people like hiring managers and senior leaders. It includes people who are instrumental in your current career activities and future career success. It also includes the people who influence those decision makers.

Doyens: These are the thought leaders in your field—the "stars" in your industry or job function. And it also includes "expertise colleagues"—others who aren't so famous but share similar knowledge or thought leadership goals. You may not share the same point of view, but you are cousins in expertise.

Disciples: These are your employees if you manage others. It can also include people you need to motivate to achieve your goals—even if you aren't their line manager. The people who follow you and those you mentor are also in this category.

Defenders: These are your go-to people for moral and professional support and guidance, including your mentors, close family, and friends. They are often the people who can help you accelerate your growth, having an impact on the speed at which you attain your goals. They can help give you the perspective you need during challenging times.

Discoursers: These are the mouthpieces with megaphones who can help you get your message heard. It includes the traditional media, authors, podcast hosts, blog owners, and social media leaders.

Now it's your turn. Take a moment to document your brand community—or 5D team, the people who need to know you so you can achieve your goals.

Once you've made a list of the people in your brand community, highlight the ones you rarely or never see in person. It takes extra effort to nurture virtual relationships. Making note of these people will help you be more intentional in your efforts to engage with them.

 FUN FACT

A 2018 study by Olivet University revealed that 76 percent of people think mentors are important, yet only 37 percent of people currently have one.

The 3 Ps Formula of Successful Branding

It's time to take a look at your brand from the outside in. Professional success doesn't happen in a vacuum. To succeed in today's ultra-competitive marketplace, you must be keenly aware of external perceptions. At CareerBlast.TV, we use the 3 Ps formula—purpose, performance, and perception—to describe what we believe it takes to be successful today (Figure 2-2).

Figure 2-2. The 3 Ps Formula of Successful Branding

Purpose + Performance + Perception = Success

Purpose: Who You Are and What Drives You

If you're not feeling fulfilled at work, it's possibly because there's a disconnect between what's important to you, what you do, and how you do it. What motivates you? What goals inspire you? When you are straightforward about your purpose, values, and your unique approach to work, you have a compass to help keep you moving in the right direction toward your ultimate vision.

Performance: How You Deliver Value at Work

This component calls for you to examine the skills required to do your job along with what it takes to get you noticed for your next role. Performance partially has to do with your technical skills, but the area that's most important when it comes to branding has to do with traits that have long been called soft skills, which reflect the human part of career success. Examining your technical skills alongside your soft skills will help you build and nurture meaningful relationships at work. Then you can make things happen.

Perception: What People Think About You

This element of the 3 Ps formula is the one that people often overlook—yet it's absolutely essential for career success. You can have clear direction and honed expertise, but if you don't have the ability to build relationships with people who count, your success will be hampered. Like it or not, our success is inextricably linked to how we are perceived by others.

Validating Your Authenticity

Whether you're searching for a new job, looking to get promoted, or seeking new clients, a complete portrait of your professional reputation is essential.

Although successful branding is based in what is authentic and genuine about you, your personal brand is held in the hearts and minds of those around you. I keep repeating that phrase because you must face these external perceptions. They help you validate self-perceptions and also provide information you can use to refine your brand.

Because these perceptions are so critical to building a truly authentic and compelling personal brand, I developed a tool to help career-minded professionals get candid feedback about how they are perceived by those around them. It's called 360Reach. But don't confuse it with 360 tools most companies use. This survey doesn't answer the question "How are you at X?" It answers the question "Who are you?"

The insights you obtain will be invaluable to your brand building. Often the insights you gain provide subtle yet powerful clues to external perceptions. I was working with a really smart and dedicated executive at a law firm. She prided herself on being the kind of leader who involves others and listens fully. When she received her 360Reach results, she realized that while some people saw her as open-minded, inclusive, and willing to consider all points of view, others saw her as wishy-washy and indecisive. Armed with this awareness, she was able to refine how she delivered her brand attributes of "open-minded and inclusive" in a way that was seen as positive and valuable to the firm.

Another client—a very senior and successful finance executive at a technology company—received one comment on her 360Reach report that forever changed the course of her career. The comment said "You're really impressive. I admire you. The only thing I don't understand is why you are in finance. You just seem like a marketer to me." Interestingly, that was always her dream—to be a CMO. But her first internship in college was in finance and she excelled in the role. Her great work led to her being hired full-time as a financial analyst. That led to other opportunities in finance and ultimately to a senior role where she was a respected and revered leader. The comment she received, though, was too much to ignore. She was passionate about marketing and wanted to pursue it. So she proposed to the CEO that she take on responsibilities for the marketing and finance of a new product that was being incubated. That move increased her happiness at work and allowed her to deliver greater value to her employer.

The message here: Get feedback from others—regularly. And take action on what you learn. You can find a complimentary version of 360Reach at http://360reach.me.

Having a tool that can help you understand your brand from the outside can really help you get a baseline understanding of external perceptions, but formally surveying people all the time is just not realistic. And the once-a-year performance evaluation summarizing what your leaders think about you is a very narrow gauge; not surprisingly, relying on those can actually impede your ability to advance rapidly. That's why you need to proactively ask for and listen to feedback from the full circle of your 5D community.

 BRAND HACK

> **Solicit regular feedback.** Overtly ask for feedback. Check in with colleagues at the end of a meeting you deliver. Ask your employees what they think you're doing well and not so well. Solicit feedback from your manager during your one-on-ones. State plainly that you encourage and appreciate candid feedback—the good, the bad, and the ugly. If the feedback doesn't jibe with your self-perception, ask yourself if this is happening because you're miscommunicating or because you haven't acknowledged a truth about yourself.

Clarity: The Key to Powerful Authenticity

Knowing your brand before crystalizing it into your unique promise of value is essential. It speaks to the first of the three Cs of personal branding: clarity. The novelist Julian Barnes is widely quoted as saying, "Mystification is simple. Clarity is the hardest thing of all." But in personal branding, the labor required to unearth the authentic you will pay off in the long run.

We'll talk about the other two Cs—consistency and constancy—in chapters 4 and 11, but for now, let's get clear about clarity (Figure 2-3).

Figure 2-3. The 3 Cs of Personal Branding

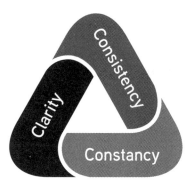

People with strong personal brands are explicit about who they are and who they're not. Being resolute about your unique promise of value is not only essential, it's an asset that pays huge dividends. It:

- helps you know what's on- and off-brand for you
- enables you to say no to things that won't help you reach your goals, giving you more time to focus on what's important
- informs how you talk about yourself to others
- makes it easier for others to spread the word about your brand on your behalf by talking to others about you
- provides a sounding board to help you make decisions about what to pursue and what not to pursue
- helps you identify topics, keywords, and points of view to include in your brand communications
- makes it a snap to write your career marketing materials
- boosts your confidence by reminding you what's unique about you
- liberates you from a hamster wheel of duties that you don't enjoy.

Summing Up

Now that your brand is firmly embedded in your mind, you have validated those self-perceptions, and know who needs to know you, it's time to put it all together so you can tell the world who you are and why they should care. Don't become the world's best-kept secret; share yourself with the world. So, it's time to tell your story. In chapter 3, we'll distill all that you learned about yourself into a story—your brand story. And you'll learn all the ways to tell that story so you can connect and engage with members of your brand community.

CHAPTER 3

Deliver Your Brand Daily

What's Your Story?

Your authentic story is told in many forms, from your elevator pitch to your bio. Dan Pink, author of *A Whole New Mind*, explains the connection between your story and authenticity brilliantly, "We are our stories. We compress years of experience, thought, and emotion into a few compact narratives that we convey to others and tell ourselves. That has always been true. But personal narrative has become more prevalent, and perhaps more urgent, in a time of abundance, when many of us are freer to seek a deeper understanding of ourselves and our purpose."

But before we get to your story, let's talk about the foundational skill that's needed to tell your story: communication.

We talked about how relationships are the currency of business. Well, communication is the foundation of fruitful relationships.

 FUN
FACT

"91 percent of employees say communication issues can drag executives down," according to an Interact/Harris poll.

Let's spend a little time on this extra-important skill.

PONDER THIS

Think about these forms of communication and give yourself a skill score from one to five. (A one means *"Yikes*, I need help with this." A five means "I'm so good at this, I could teach others.")

Listening		1 2 3 4 5
Writing (long form)		1 2 3 4 5
Email		1 2 3 4 5
Public speaking		1 2 3 4 5
Telephone		1 2 3 4 5
In-person discussion		1 2 3 4 5
Texting/IMing		1 2 3 4 5
Video		1 2 3 4 5
Social media		1 2 3 4 5

How were your scores? If you scored a three or lower in any area, it's time for a workout to strengthen that zone. All of the communication forms on this list are crucial in today's world of work.

To get stronger in any of these areas, your resources include hiring a coach, asking HR to offer a professional development session, enrolling in a short-term professional development course (they're even available online), and seeking a role model. Whose social media posts do you look forward to reading? Who writes the best pitch letters in your department? Who's the best listener you know?

MINDSET RESET

Despite its pervasiveness, email is often not the right vehicle for effective communication. Ditch the default and determine the most appropriate vehicle for each communication you have to deliver. Then stand out not only by what you say, but also by the means you use to say it.

If you've identified a communication skill that you need to work on, you're already starting to work toward making an improvement. That's because if you identify a need for improvement, you will become more aware of the maestros around you, and you can start taking note of what makes their delivery so appealing. If you do enroll in a short course, you can add that to your resume. And if you hire a coach, that person will become part of your network. You have nothing to lose and much to gain by strengthening this fundamental skill.

FUN FACT

According to the technology marketing firm Radicati Group, the number of emails sent daily will exceed 333 billion by 2022.

Tell Your Story

All strong brands are clear about their story, and all strong brand managers can tell that story to a variety of people using various communications vehicles. The first step is defining your story. That means taking what you learned about your brand when you took time for introspection in chapter 1, combined with the feedback from others, and deciding which elements to include as part of your narrative. The technique I use with all my clients involves gathering the raw data and using it to fill six "content buckets."

The Six Content Buckets

These six categories of content will help you identify the elements of your story: accomplishments, values and passions, superpowers, differentiation, quantifiable facts, and validation.

Accomplishments

Craft a sentence for each of your most important accomplishments in terms of the value you create or created. Remember "nexting," the trend discussed in the introduction—include those accomplishments that are most relevant to what you want to do next.

Values and Passions

Your answers to the Ponder This questions in chapter 1 will help you here. Just remember to edit. It's not about adding all your values and passions; select only the ones that are important to expressing your brand.

Superpowers

These are your signature strengths. What do you do better than anyone else? What skills do you possess that are rare?

Differentiation

This is the moment when your quirks get to shine. What appealing aspects of your background, your work process, your life story, and your personality (the sky's the limit!) help you stand out from others?

Quantifiable Facts

Make your accomplishments count, literally. Sales figures, budget savings, number of presentations, frequent flier miles accrued in a year: It all adds up.

Validation

Quotes, awards, testimonials, and accolades bestowed upon you from someone else or by an organization—like being quoted in a publication—along with your degrees will serve to confirm what you're saying about yourself.

Once you have filled your content buckets, ask yourself these two questions:

- **Is there anything missing?** If so, just add it in. Maybe there was a detail that didn't seem to fit in any bucket. Find a place for it regardless.
- **Is there anything extraneous?** When you look at all your facts and figures together, are there some things that are just not as important as the rest? If so, remove them. You need to deliver a cohesive message, not a cornucopia of unrelated tidbits.

Now you have everything you need to be able to tell your story.

BRANDI BRAINSTORMS

This is how Brandi, our example personal brander, filled her content buckets:

Accomplishments

I built a new project management format for my department to streamline the data analysis process. Built and led the market research team with the lowest attrition in the organization. Mentored our intern, and now he's one of our best new hires.

Values and Passions

Curiosity (I have to know why), creativity (no one ever sees me wearing black), collaboration, team sports (I was on the women's basketball team in college), and travel to Asia.

Superpowers

Harmony: I inspire teams to exceed client expectations by getting past their differences of opinion and focusing on a vision and shared mission. My nickname at work is The Persuader. I can convince even the most skeptical product manager of the importance of using social media tools like Twitter and Instagram.

Differentiation

I like to challenge the status quo and say things in meetings that makes people stop and think. I use my international expertise and passion for travel to design truly global advertising campaigns. Many people in the world focus on assimilating. I'm OK with standing out. Oh, and my name is spelled with an "i," which is unusual for my name. In my signature, I like to turn that "i" into a tiny exclamation point.

Quantifiable Facts

I climbed two of the world's tallest peaks. I lived in five countries and speak three languages—French, English, and Spanish. I implemented marketing campaigns that reeled in $500,000 of additional business while reducing our media spend by 20 percent.

Validation
Graduated cum laude from the University of Massachusetts. Was named in the top 10 marketers to follow on Twitter.

If your buckets aren't as full as Brandi's, don't despair. Her list didn't always look like this, but she did a great job of nurturing the seeds she started with.

Now let's start writing. When it comes to branding, your story comes in three sizes: Small. Medium. Large.

The Small: Tagline

You can use your tagline to describe your brand promise or convey your brand personality. Taglines are powerful because they can encapsulate an entire image into a few words. But they need to be memorable.

Smart. Fun. Funny. Fearless.

That was the tagline of *Spy* magazine, a satirical monthly published in the eighties and nineties. It was the brainchild of Kurt Andersen and Graydon Carter. Although the magazine might be extinct, you may have heard of it through references during the 2016 presidential campaign. That's because *Spy* magazine had once called Donald Trump a "short-fingered vulgarian," which became part of the sophomoric hand-size comparisons between Donald Trump and Marco Rubio during one of the debates. That irreverence was part of the magazine's DNA, brilliantly summed up in its four-word, 27-character tagline. And the message in the tagline proved to have enduring truth.

Your tagline can be a statement, a promise, or a series of attributes.

BRANDI
BRAINSTORMS
Brandi came up with three tagline options for herself:
- I always want to know why. And then I figure out how.
- Persuasive. Persistent. Passionate.
- The world is an open door, if you have the right keys.

Here are two compelling real-world taglines:

- *I spend my days making sure our talent has the skills, support, and sparkle they need to be the best in the industry.*
- *I'm a data explorer. I can grow your business by driving deeper understanding through data analytics.*

Your tagline can also be something that was bestowed on you by someone else. I use "the personal branding guru," which was how *Entrepreneur* magazine referred to me . . . because as I tell everyone, I'm a one-trick pony. Personal branding is my thing!

The Medium: Elevator Pitch

Every time you meet someone in person or are in a meeting where not everyone knows everyone else, you'll share your elevator pitch. All effective elevator pitches share these qualities. They're:

- **Brief.** Think of the elevator in an office-park building, not an elevator in the Empire State Building.
- **Relevant.** Your elevator pitch changes slightly to adapt to the person or people you're meeting.
- **Intriguing.** Not the kind of dramatic intrigue you'd get in a John Grisham novel, but the kind that makes people want to know more about you.

The problem with most elevator pitches is that they are boring and set the speaker up to be a commodity. That's because most people don't introduce themselves by what sets them apart. Instead, they focus on their job function, title, and company—what makes them blend in. That's not branding—that's conforming.

The Large: Branded Bio

Today, your most important career document is your bio—or what I like to call your branded bio. The resume used to be the tool that would get you noticed. No more. It's still an important career asset, but it's been relegated to being a document merely used for proof.

Your most valuable branding document is the 3D brand bio. It's you in 3D. It should be refined for your LinkedIn summary, your corporate website, your intro when you give speeches, and everywhere else that people are going to receive their first impression of you.

Use first-person point of view (I/me) for your 3D brand bio. You can create versions in the third person (he/him, she/her, or they/them) where it's more appropriate. The first person is powerful because it is more transparent and personal—and when someone reads your bio, it's like having a conversation with you.

To draft your 3D brand bio, weave elements from the six content categories into a compelling narrative that touts what makes you great. Combining elements from the different categories throughout your summary makes it more interesting.

Then, close with a call to action.

You'll use your bio throughout the rest of this book as your source document for crafting your story for the digital world.

MINDSET RESET

Professional bios are not just for celebrities, authors, and senior executives. Whether you're a high school student seeking admission into your favorite university or an intellectual property lawyer working for a pharmaceutical firm, you need a professional bio.

Make Your Mark in Meetings

Depending on your role, you can spend between 30 to 50 percent of your work time in meetings. So it's easy to see that one of the best personal branding opportunities occurs in the meeting room (or in the case of remote workers, in the Zoom room).

The most common mistake professionals make when it comes to meetings is ignoring the prep. When you don't prepare for a meeting "because you just have to show up to this one," notice the red flag waving wildly in your face. Either don't waste your precious time going (that is, delegate attendance to someone else) or prepare to show up with a real presence. My CareerBlast.TV co-founder and NYC-based executive coach, Ora, provides this advice for the perfect prep:

- Review background materials or do a bit of research on the topic.
- Formulate an initial point of view (your branded perspective) on the topic.
- Analyze the audience who will be present. What are their perspectives? What are the hot buttons when it comes to this topic? Who's the key decision maker?
- Ask: How do I want the audience to feel about me after the meeting?

While there's been much talk about where the most powerful seat is around the table and how to look assertive on video conference, Ora declares that every and any seat can be the power seat if you focus on two things: your nonverbal and your verbal communication.

When it comes to having presence nonverbally, start by sitting assertively, whether you're in the flesh or on video. Lose the distracting e-device, lean in physically, and make eye contact (or look directly into the camera lens). If you're small physically, take up more space by raising your seat, resting your hands on the table, and yes . . . gently airing out your armpits (try it and you'll get it).

✔ **DO THIS,**
✘ **NOT THAT**

Do participate in meetings beyond just delivering your update. Be present and engaged for the entire meeting.	**Don't** sit back and relax in meetings, or worse, get on your device when others are sharing their updates.

Your verbal communication at the meeting is what will help you make your mark. If you're relatively junior or know zilch about the topic, remind yourself that people deep in the weeds of a problem or solution often miss the big picture. Here's your opportunity!

 BRAND
HACK

> **Ask a question.** When you're in a meeting, struggling to come up with something valuable to say, listen closely, and then ask a strategic question. For example:
> - What's the risk of ignoring the problem?
> - Have we looked at alternative solutions?
> - Do we have benchmark data on how others are handling this?
> - If we invest now, when do we expect to see a ROI?

To make matters even simpler, Ora suggests you can ask the very same question in every meeting. She calls it the branded question. This question reflects your deeply developed point of view or value.

If you're like most professionals, you're often asked to give an update of your work at meetings, and this is another perfect opportunity for you to make your mark. Instead of talking just about what you've done and the challenges you face, talk about the results of your actions. In other words, talk about what you've achieved to date. If you haven't progressed much on the given goal, Ora advises you talk about why the launch was successful, why the initial baby steps situate you for big success, or what great results you expect. And if you are indeed facing big challenges, problems, barriers, and obstacles, that's OK and perfectly common. But if you want to show up with senior presence at meetings, make sure you don't just whine about your problems. Focus on offering up some alternative solutions for discussion.

Finally, yet another way Ora suggests to power up your meeting presence is to offer your opinions and perspectives. Why keep them in your head and then kick yourself when someone else offers them up? Coach Ora recommends you get courageous and break into the conversation with a simple question: May I add my perspective here? If you balance curiosity (listening and asking questions) with advocacy (offering your opinion) you'll never get in trouble. On the contrary, you'll show up as adding significant value at every meeting while bolstering your brand. And that influences perception. Along with performance, it's perception that will get you promoted!

REMOTE CONTROL

Participating remotely can make meetings more challenging from a branding perspective. Here's how to make sure you get noticed:

- If leading the meeting, make it a video meeting. It's the next best thing to being there. Don't be tempted to opt for a phone conference. If you're not the lead, try to get the leader to use Zoom, Skype, or Google Hangouts.
- Make sure people know who you are—when appropriate, precede your brilliant contributions with your name.
- Make your mark. Commit to leaving the meeting having contributed in a memorable way.

Integrating your brand into meetings, as these examples show, is easy—and what's more, essential. I once worked with an accounting executive at a tech firm. Her brand was all about creativity, but she was one of few at her workplace who knew that. Why? Because she told herself that there's no room for creativity when you work in accounting. She got her fill of creativity outside the office by drawing, painting, doing interior design, and creating her own recipes, but that meant she had established a firm separation between work and life. It was less than ideally fulfilling. So I challenged her. I told her that if she's so creative, she could surely find a creative way to integrate her brand into what she does. She accepted the challenge and decided to focus on leading meetings because they take up the most time in her weekly calendar.

Here's how it played out.

She dissected a meeting into its individual components:

- invitation
- agenda
- kickoff
- introductions
- discussion
- recap/closing
- follow-up.

Then for each element, she integrated her creativity. For example, her meeting invitations were sent on fun stationery she drew by hand and then converted to a Word template. (Digital stationery is great for branding, by the way.) The agenda was always delivered in a format that was fun—like a word search or a crossword puzzle or a mnemonic so attendees could remember the topics. She did this for all aspects of all meetings, and a couple of interesting things happened. She found that she actually enjoys leading meetings. And . . . she found that people liked her meetings so much, people who had no reason to attend were clamoring to get in.

Now it's your turn. Meetings are often the most powerful business activity for brand building—but not always. Identify the business action that sits at the center of these three elements:

- **High frequency:** You do it a lot.
- **Visibility:** It gives you the opportunity to be seen by others.
- **Enjoyment:** You get satisfaction from doing it.

It could be leading meetings, but it might also be giving client pitch presentations, participating in team updates, or creating project status reports.

Now, break that activity into its components. Stir your special sauce into each one of them and watch your level of involvement soar.

 PONDER THIS

Before every meeting you attend, ask yourself these questions:
- How do my project goals align to and support my company's business goals?
- Which key members of my brand community will be there?
- What contribution can I make that will allow me to showcase my brand?
- How can I acknowledge others and express gratitude and praise?

Summing Up

Chapter 3 was all about the power of storytelling. We discussed the different forms your story takes and the different venues where you can tell that story and attract the attention of decision makers. Now, in part 2, it's time to translate that real-world narrative into your digital brand. In chapter 4, you'll take the first step by understanding why digital branding is essential (thanks to the digital-first phenomenon) and by establishing your baseline through time-tested tools.

Part 2
Virtual You

PART 2

Virtual You

Now that you have clarity about the real you, you're ready for part 2: the process of translating that information into the virtual version of you! We'll achieve that by first understanding where your brand currently stands online. That baseline will help you build your digital-branding strategy, which is rooted in three essential elements:

- **profile:** the first impression you deliver
- **people:** your network and target audience
- **performance:** enhancing your success by growing your brand.

In chapter 4, I'll introduce you to the digital-first phenomenon. Then, in chapter 5, I'll share with you why—regardless of your role, level, industry, or organization—your LinkedIn profile is the most important digital branding tool you have for delivering your first impression and forming a foundation for building relationships. And I'll help you get a handle on what your current profile says about you. Chapter 6 is focused on my proven step-by-step process for building a truly stellar LinkedIn profile—and we'll start thinking about how you can apply what you've learned to other social media.

CHAPTER 4

Understand the Digital-First Phenomenon

Enchanté

When I was living in Paris, I loved meeting new people—partly because I just love meeting people. My fascination with people is partly why I have devoted my career to the field of personal branding. I particularly loved meeting new people in France because when you're introduced to someone new, their response is "Enchanté." Of course, translated into English, it means "nice to meet you" (literally, "I'm enchanted by you") but the word *enchanté* is so much more powerful than that. The English word *enchanted*, according to Dictionary.com, means "delighted to a high degree."

When someone meets you, don't you want them to be delighted to a high degree? Don't you want your first impression to be enchanting?

Well, that's what I want for you, and in this chapter, we'll discuss what you need to do to create an authentic, relevant, and—yes—enchanting first impression. And that first impression needs to be just as powerful in the virtual world. Why?

Because first impressions have gone digital (remember trend number 3 from the introduction).

**MINDSET
RESET**

Your first impression is more and more likely to be formed online. That means your digital brand needs to be as magnetic, human, and engaging as the real you. There was a time when online branding was a nice-to-have instead of an absolute must. Today, your virtual brand has become your calling card.

From Handshake to Handheld Device

In the past, most first impressions were formed in real-world connections, often with a handshake. After an initial meeting, we might search the web to learn more about those we had met. That paradigm has flipped: the in-person handshake is now the second or even third impression, if it happens at all (many remote workers have never met their colleagues in person). My assistant Deborah (or the world's most impressive assistant, as I call her) and I worked together for six years before we ever met in person. This phenomenon—coined "digital first" by Mitch Joel in his book *Ctrl Alt Delete*—means you need to be steadfastly focused on your digital brand if you want to master your first impression.

> *"You never get a second chance to make a first impression."*
> —often attributed to Will Rogers

People are learning about you online before they ever meet you in person, and they're making decisions about you based on who Google says you are. The instant they know they're going to meet you or have a call with you, they'll type your name into Google and see what shows up. I call it she-surfing or he-surfing:

> *She-surf/He-surf (v): The act of typing the name of someone into Google for the purpose of learning about them.*

Even in companies with robust intranets, employees learn about their colleagues through Google searches. In my corporate workshops I routinely ask participants this question:

"Have you ever googled someone in this company?"

Without exception, nearly every hand goes up. Then I say:

"Keep your hand up if you have googled someone in this room."

And typically more than half the hands remain raised.

This means that you need to make the real you congruent with the virtual you. And you must be able to tell your story online in 3D, creating a magnetic, complete picture of who you are and what makes you great. Recall in chapter 2, where I introduced the three Cs of personal branding (Figure 4-1) and discussed the importance of the first C, clarity? The essential congruence I'm talking about here refers to the second C in the three Cs of strong brands—consistency. With every interaction with others, you must deliver a consistent, branded experience.

Figure 4-1. The 3 Cs of Personal Branding

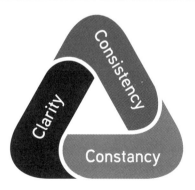

Think about Starbucks. Whether you walk into a Starbucks in New York, New Delhi, or Newfoundland you'll get your venti, nonfat, no foam, extra-hot latte—and have a similar experience no matter which location you choose. And when you think about Apple, the experiences you have in an Apple store, on the website, and when you're communicating with a customer-support professional over the phone are similar. You need to think of the experience you create for others in the same way—that means building consistency between the real and virtual you.

Beware of Bias

There are three important cognitive biases to consider when it comes to mastering your first impression: primacy, confirmation, and anchoring (Figure 4-2).

Figure 4-2. Cognitive Biases

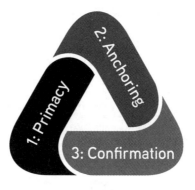

Cognitive Bias 1: Primacy

Primacy essentially means that we believe the first thing we learn. Primacy is the reason **first impressions matter.**

 REMOTE CONTROL

Be deliberate when meeting people for the first time. Make a special effort to convey your brand when meeting new people from a distance. Research people before you meet them and find common connections. Go out of your way to deliver your brand.

Cognitive Bias 2: Anchoring

The second bias is anchoring—and this is where things get serious. Anchoring means that once we form a first impression, it becomes anchored in our thinking, making it hard for us to change our mind.

Anchoring is the reason **first impressions last.**

Imagine this scenario:

A senior leader sees your name on the attendee list for an upcoming meeting, and she googles you to learn about you only to discover a hodge-podge of conflicting information. Her first impression is that you're scatterbrained. But when she connects with you in the meeting, you're focused and impeccably organized, nothing like your Google results. Guess what? She may not believe the flesh-and-bones you she just met. Instead, she'll focus on the less-than-impressive bits-and-bytes you she met first online.

Cognitive Bias 3: Confirmation

Confirmation bias speaks to the cumulative effect of information and interactions. When you make a great first impression, and the next inter-action or two (whether online or in the real world) are equally positive and consistent with your first impression, you essentially can do no wrong.

It works the other way too.

An unimpressive online presence followed by a lackluster real-world interaction sets the expectation on a negative path.

Confirmation bias is the reason **real** and **virtual** impressions can become deal breakers.

This means that if you want to build strong and enduring relationships with others, every interaction, piece of information, and bit of feedback must reinforce your authentic brand and how you want to be known.

Found in Translation

The digital branding process is not a separate branding activity; it's an exercise in translation.

The questions to ask are:

- How do I translate the flesh-and-bones me into the bits-and-bytes me?
- How do I make sure the real and the virtual work together to keep me visible, available, and valuable to the people who are making decisions about me?

Those are the questions you'll answer as we sail ahead in this *Digital You* journey.

As you saw, the previous section of this book had nothing to do with online branding. That's because you can't build a powerful digital brand until you're crystal clear about your authentic real-world brand. That's why the tag line for this book is *Real Personal Branding in the Virtual Age*. Once your real-world brand is defined, you can transform it for the online world—keeping it accurate, authentic, and relevant. We'll begin that real-to-virtual translation process now by discovering exactly what your current online brand says about you.

Now that you know why digital branding is essential to success, it's time to create your strategy for building your virtual brand. Start with the 50,000-foot view before working on individual virtual branding activities like building your LinkedIn profile or growing your Twitter following.

Where do most great journeys start?

With an understanding of where you are today.

The rest of this chapter is devoted to assessing where you are so we can make a plan to get you where you need to be. Specifically, we'll focus on understanding what Google says about you.

Your Google Quotient and Online ID

If you don't show up in Google, do you exist?

When someone googles you, they evaluate you on five measures of online branding. They don't realize they're doing this, but it's how they make sense of your Google results. I'll refer to these five measures throughout the rest of this book as we talk about the tactics you can use to master your online brand.

Let's discuss each of the five measures briefly, starting with volume and relevance. These two measures are critical to online branding, and they set up this model (Figure 4-3). And as with most four-box models, the goal is to be in the upper right quadrant—in this case, it means being digitally distinct.

Figure 4-3. Volume and Relevance

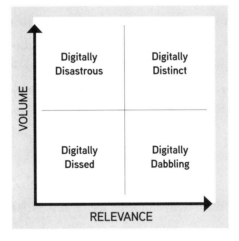

Volume

This is a quantitative measure. It speaks to how much content you have on the web. Lots of content means "This person must have something to say." No content or little content sends the opposite message.

Relevance

This is a qualitative measure. When someone googles you, they're asking one of these questions: "Do I need to know this person?" or "Is this the person I thought they were?" Success in both areas requires that you be relevant and compelling to your stakeholders.

Purity

This is especially important for people with common names or who share names with celebrities. It focuses on your ability to stand out from others who have the same name. So what do you do if you have a common name—or worse, you share your name with a celebrity? Later in this chapter, we'll talk about proven strategies to distinguish yourself.

Diversity

This measure has to do with the format of your online content. Is it all text-based, or are there images, videos, presentations, and documents to help support and amplify your message? The greater the diversity of media, the greater your impact. I will share effective, easy-to-implement techniques later in the book.

Validation

Since we could all spend our time pounding our virtual chests and creating content to increase the volume of search results, we need something to validate what we say about ourselves. This validation is provided by external sources and typically comes in the form of testimonials, recommendations, endorsements, awards, and accolades. If everything on the web about you comes directly from you, viewers are incredulous. But when your self-proclamations are reinforced by the words of others, they become credible.

I spoke of these five measures of online branding over a decade ago in my first book, *Career Distinction*. Back then, I didn't have nearly as much data as I do today. Now I'm able to share the insights I have gleaned from hundreds of thousands of data points. These insights can help you see how you fare compared to others in your peer group.

Insights From the Online ID Calculator

Here's some of what we learned from nearly 100,000 pieces of data from users of the Online ID Calculator.

CEOs Are Not the Most Visible

Although you might expect CEOs to be the most prominent and polished online presences because of the opportunities they have to visible, it's not the case. It's the younger generations—those who grew up with their fingers attached to keys and their heads gazing at their mobile devices—who are most visible online.

Entry-level employees responded "yes" most often to the question "Did video of you show up in your search results?" That was followed by individual contributors with some experience. CEOs came in third.

Their natural tendency to live their lives online can have a negative impact on the careers of entry-level and individual contributors as well. These two job-level categories were the groups who acknowledged that they have digital dirt (I explain digital dirt below).

When it comes to being digitally distinct, the top five job levels of our users to receive this score were:

1. individual contributor
2. managers
3. entry level
4. directors
5. CEOs.

Although CEOs don't have the volume of results we see with younger users of the tool, they are also less likely to be digitally disastrous. Their content has a high relevance score. CEOs came in last for scores on digitally disastrous.

Marketers Are Most Digitally Distinct

Those in marketing—not surprisingly—came out on top with the highest percentage of users in the digitally distinct category, followed by entrepreneurs, then those in engineering.

Engineers showed up in the digitally disastrous category as well—at the top, followed by those in marketing then salespeople. We found this surprising since salespeople are usually focused on making powerful, positive first impressions.

There Are Gender Differences

Women had less content on the web than their male counterparts, with almost 30 percent more of them receiving the score digitally dabbling. Women were also less likely to have digital dirt and less likely to have video show up in their Google results.

We are going to continue to track the data from the Online ID Calculator to see how new technologies, new trends, and new generations affect the results.

Get Your Quotient

OK. Are you ready to establish your baseline?

It's time to ego surf or narcissurf—that's what it's called when you google yourself—to determine your current Google Quotient.

- Go to the CareerBlast Online ID Calculator
  (www.onlineidcalculator.com).

- With a computer and a browser that you rarely use, visit the websites that come up with a Google search of your name. Ego surf.
- Follow the Online ID Calculator directions and see your results in the five measures of online ID.

How did you do?

Remember, you used this calculator to establish your baseline. It doesn't matter if you were digitally distinct or digitally disastrous. In upcoming chapters, I'll share with you everything you need to do so you can move the needle on your virtual brand score. But first, a message about housecleaning.

Ditch the Digital Dirt

One of the questions I am asked regularly at the end of a keynote is:

"What do I do if a Google search displays unwanted content about me?"

If your search results reveal digital dirt—things that are unflattering, untrue, or just inconsistent with how you want to be known so you can achieve your goals—there's good news.

People rarely go beyond page one in a Google search (or one screen's worth of content on a mobile device), and they almost never go beyond page three. So all you need to do is focus intently on page one and a little on pages two and three.

 FUN
FACT

According to data from the Online ID Calculator, more junior employees are likely to have digital dirt, with entry-level employees saying they have digital dirt more than any other group.

There's more good news! It's easier than you think to diminish the downside of digital dirt. Just as with most messes, there are two ways to clean it up.

Vacuum it up. That means either take down the undesirable content if you're the one who put it up, or speak to the owners of the sites where it appears and ask them to remove it.

Sweep it under the rug. This is what you do with content you can't get removed. Because people spend most of their time evaluating you with the first page or two of your results, the goal is to get your name featured in lots of positive, current, high-ranking content to push the digital dirt down. The content can of course include web pages you control, such as your personal website or your LinkedIn profile.

BRAND HACK

Stay on top of your Google results. Set up a Google alert for your name at alerts.google.com. Put your name in quotes like this: "William Arruda". This way, when your name appears on the web you'll know about it.

What's in a Name?

When your parents named you, they probably weren't thinking about any web confusion they would cause if they didn't choose a unique name like Tangerine or Moon Unit. So some of us are stuck with common names, or we share our name with someone famous or prolific on the web.

FUN FACT

According to howmanyofme.com, there are 30,677 people named John Williams and 11,492 people named Susan Smith in the United States. There are 1,033 James Bonds, 51 Julianne Moores, 18 Olivia Popes, and 53 Jackie Chans.

Here's the good news.

People have become sophisticated searchers. They know that they need to refine the search when they see content that just doesn't seem right. And refine it they will. That means they'll put in a word or phrase to filter out the "un-you" content. The trick? You need to know the keywords they'll use, and you need to make sure you include those distinguishing keywords in everything you post on the web.

I'm fortunate because I have a fairly distinctive name—my last name is an uncommon Portuguese word, and there are not many Portuguese people named William. Despite this good fortune, I know that my results might not always stay pure. So I make sure everything I post online has the term "personal branding" in it. Virtually every one of the more than 300 articles in my *Forbes* column contains that phrase, as do my LinkedIn blogs, YouTube video tags, and other components of my digital footprint.

What Are Your Keywords?

Take a moment now to identify your keywords. If you're not already clear about the keywords for which you want to be known, here are four ways to identify the right words or phrases for you:

Review your message. Go back to part 1 of this book and review the section where you defined your message or point of view. What words did you use to describe your unique message?

Put yourself in your stakeholders' shoes. Think about the people you are looking to influence. Who are the decision makers? Then think about the words and phrases they would use if they were looking for you or someone who does what you do.

Research job listings. Find at least five job listings on LinkedIn, Indeed, and so on for the role you have, and five for the role you seek to have (remember, personal branding is both authentic and aspirational). Then look for the keywords these listings have in common.

Look up your colleagues. Search LinkedIn for people who have your job title and people who have the job title you would like to hold next. Record the keywords you see that are common to these profiles.

Linking It All Back to LinkedIn

Now you have a baseline understanding of where your digital brand stands today along with some strategies for eliminating digital dirt, making sure people can find you in a sea of others with your name, and determining which keywords are the most relevant to your goals. It's time to focus on one particular Google result—your LinkedIn profile.

When it comes to your professional image, your digital first impression comes from your LinkedIn profile. Why?

When someone is checking you out in a professional capacity, they often start at LinkedIn. But even if they start at Google, it's highly likely that your LinkedIn profile will show up in one of the top three spots because LinkedIn meets so many of the criteria in Google's algorithm for high-ranking search. And 61 percent of all clicks go to those top three spots.

This is great news. It means that you have one primary tool to help you build your first virtual first impression. I hope that takes some pressure off. Phew!

Summing Up

In chapter 4, you learned why digital branding is so important—it often delivers your first impression—and I introduced you to some tools that help you get clear about where your bits-and-bytes brand stands right now. That understanding is important because you will be able to see how you impact your digital branding with the actions we discuss throughout the rest of this book. In chapter 5, we are going to take a deep dive into the most important professional social network: LinkedIn. I'll share a tool you can use to evaluate your LinkedIn profile along with the new mindset you need to adopt to make the most of this digital branding powerhouse.

CHAPTER 5

Use LinkedIn As Your First Impression

Stand Out Online

I must come clean right up front. I am LinkedIn's biggest fan. I am so sanguine about LinkedIn, people think I own a lot of stock in their parent company (Microsoft) or I work for them (that part is true: I have done work for them in the past). But my excitement for LinkedIn is actually rooted in my passion for personal branding.

I'm an unexpected entrepreneur, having held roles in corporate branding for the first chapter of my adult life. I only stopped "working for the man" because I was so passionate about the idea of personal branding. If there had been a role for a chief personal branding officer, I would have stayed in the corporate world for the rest of my career. But that wasn't the case. These days, my work has evolved to focus mostly on digital branding, and LinkedIn has become the primary tool my corporate clients deploy.

Why LinkedIn?

There are literally hundreds of online branding tools you can use to increase your visibility and grow your personal brand, but trying to work on all of them would take too much time; focus is critical. I recommend you start with only one tool—and for most of us, that tool is LinkedIn. You'll find that it's the place people go, and it has become valuable to companies.

It's the Place People Go

LinkedIn is often the first place people go when they want to learn about you in a professional capacity. It's assumed that all professionals who are serious about their careers have a LinkedIn profile. How would you feel about someone you met at a networking event whom you discovered didn't have a LinkedIn profile? Would you be skeptical? And if people are researching you through a Google search, they'll likely end up at your LinkedIn profile because, as I mentioned in the last chapter, Google's algorithm often bumps sites like LinkedIn to the top, so your LinkedIn profile will typically show up in one of the top three spots on the results page—and that's where most of the clicks happen.

It Has Become Valuable to Companies

Once upon a time, companies were leery of their people being on LinkedIn. Bosses feared it was only used by people who were looking to jump ship. Today, companies are encouraging their people to use LinkedIn because they know it does a lot more than help individuals to advance their career—it helps the company, too. We'll talk about this in detail in chapter 12.

Adopting a New Mindset

In working with professionals, from C-suite leaders to entry-level employees, I have learned that when it comes to LinkedIn, everyone wants to start with the sexy stuff—reaching out to build a network of connections and posting content for others to see. That's all great (and we'll talk about that in the upcoming sections of the book). But doing that before you polish your profile will work against you. You need to start by building a powerful, magnetic, and (of course) authentic profile. That's what delivers your first impression and serves as the foundation for all the other activities you will pursue in LinkedIn.

When LinkedIn was born in 2003, it was a service with incredible potential, but for the most part, it served two primary purposes: to provide a digital version of your resume, and to be a platform for virtual networking. Its key focus was job searching.

LinkedIn became the place you absolutely needed to be if you're looking for a job. It also came with a double-edged sword. Back then, creating your LinkedIn profile was met with trepidation by LinkedIn members: "I don't want my manager thinking I am looking for a job." And it was met with suspicion from the other side: "If my people are on LinkedIn, they must be looking to leave."

If you still think of LinkedIn in these terms, you're stuck in 2003. In this world, *Friends* is the number 1 TV show, the Concorde is still flying, and Arnold Schwarzenegger was just elected governor of California.

The most pernicious byproduct with this mindset is that it made LinkedIn binary. Because of the job search focus, it became a place you didn't visit very often. Sure, if you were looking for a job or had a major career event—like a promotion or a new job—you'd visit your profile to update it. But back then, you rarely went into LinkedIn, and you surely didn't visit your profile daily.

Now that LinkedIn has matured, you must adopt a new mindset about the site.

Although LinkedIn is still used as a job search and recruiting tool, its greatest value comes from the features that allow you to learn and grow, and to become a part of communities. Most of these features have been added over the past several years. Together, they make LinkedIn the single most valuable digital branding tool you have—besides yourself, of course.

It's not just about being found. LinkedIn also ticks all the boxes when it comes to online branding. There's little you can't do with LinkedIn when it comes to showcasing your expertise, increasing visibility, and nurturing your network. We'll talk a lot about this in the next chapter and in part 4 of the book. I will share with you my favorite tips, tricks, and techniques for maximizing LinkedIn.

MINDSET RESET

LinkedIn's primary value comes from helping you do your job better and deliver greater value to your employer.

To get the most out of that value, you still have to start by focusing on LinkedIn's role in delivering your first impression. Your profile is you when you aren't there. Since LinkedIn is the place people (including current co-workers) go to learn about you, it's an opportunity to be visible to decision makers—being found by people who need to know you. With all the features it offers to personalize your profile, you can paint a portrait of the value you deliver in a differentiated and compelling way. It is a living virtual document that grows with you, becoming a comprehensive collection of your most important wins and giving you access to knowledge that will help you score those wins. But no matter how you're using it, LinkedIn delivers your first impression.

Sure, there are lots of social networks that help you remain visible to your target audience, express your point of view, and be part of an interconnected community. And many of them will be valuable to you in building your digital brand. You need to determine which media are right for you based on where your target audience goes for information and how that audience likes to communicate. (We'll talk about other social media tools in part 4.) But for every career-minded professional, until another social media platform comes along to replace it, LinkedIn is the essential site.

**FUN
FACT**

There are more than half a billion members of LinkedIn as of this writing, so it's the largest professional network in the world—and the only one that operates everywhere. In China, Facebook and Twitter are banned.

As more people understand the tremendous value in LinkedIn, that number will grow.

Now before you build that brilliant profile, let's take a big-picture look at LinkedIn. Then you'll be ready to craft your profile in chapter 6.

✔ **DO THIS,**
✘ **NOT THAT**

Do think of LinkedIn as *you* when you can't be there in person.	**Don't** think of LinkedIn as a resume.

LinkedIn: Your Personal Branding Team

LinkedIn has quickly transformed into a rich, customizable, multifaceted personal branding platform. LinkedIn can become your powerful partner in long-range branding and career management. Here are all the functions it adds to your team—without having to add to your payroll:

It's your agent. Often delivering the first impression to a prospect, your LinkedIn profile is you when you aren't there.

It's your business developer. Replete with the right keywords, your LinkedIn profile attracts and connects you with people who need what you have to offer. You may not know who might be looking for you, but a profile packed with the right search terms will help you get found. It's called "planned serendipity."

It's your professional association. It allows you to be part of the right communities and conversations. More and more, you need to be connected to others who share your expertise and interests. LinkedIn groups and other features make it efficient for you to be part of targeted discussions so you can remain current and participate even more than you could with your local professional association.

It's your publicist. Move over, CNN. LinkedIn lets you showcase your expertise and express your point of view. Through the way you write your summary to the content you share in your activity feed, the groups you join, and the conversations you have, you can tell people who you are and what you believe.

It's your graphic designer. It helps you paint a 3D portrait of the value you create. LinkedIn now allows you to integrate images or videos into your profile summary and experience, making it a true multimedia portfolio of who you are, what you have to offer, and why your work is valuable.

It's your reference check. By allowing your community to applaud your accomplishments, LinkedIn provides validation for everything you say about yourself. Endorsements help confirm your strengths and skills. Recommendations allow you to put the spotlight on testimonials that are associated with your various roles.

It's your mentor. It helps you learn and grow. LinkedIn Influencers and Topics help you stay on top of news and ideas, as well as the wisdom of key influencers. Groups also allow you to stay current about relevant and timely issues, and they help you build relationships with people who can guide you in your career decisions.

It's your recruiter. LinkedIn not only helps others find you, it helps you find the ideal people you need for those open positions on your team.

It's your salesperson. If you're looking to get in to see a client or potential business partner, your complete and compelling profile can make the difference between being invited to pitch and having a door closed in your face.

It's your contact manager. It allows you to organize and manage all the people in your professional life. You can add your email and phone contacts to your LinkedIn connections—making it the only tool you need to find the key players in your community, even when they switch jobs and their email address changes.

It's your researcher. Whether you are looking to learn about a new field, want to see who the experts are in a specific industry, or would like to know more about a particular company or product, LinkedIn gives you the 4-1-1.

Perfecting Your Profile

Now that you're convinced of the value of LinkedIn, let's focus on perfecting your profile.

 BRAND HACK

Go from boring to branded. If you think of your profile as a mere resume, it will become nothing more than a proof tool—a list of facts. But when you think of it as a career portfolio, it becomes a vivid, memorable 3D portrait of who you are, what makes you great, and why people should care.

Before you start creating your profile, evaluate where you are. There are two important attributes that make your profile powerful: credibility and likability.

Do You Know Your Credibility Score?

Credibility is critical. If you aren't credible, you're disposable. Your credibility rises as you prove that you are who you are and you do what you say you're going to do. And you can truly boost your credibility when you can tout the acknowledgment and respect of others—especially those who are revered in your area of expertise.

PONDER THIS

Get your credibility score by ranking yourself on a scale of 1-5 on the following questions:

- Are you respected? Does your profile include external validation of what you say about yourself (recommendations from high-profile leaders, references to quotes of you in publications)?
- Are your top three endorsements tied to the skills for which you want to be known?
- Does your profile include blog posts, media, and other items that demonstrate your skills?
- Is your profile expertly written, free of grammatical and spelling errors, and pleasing to look at because it contains the right amount of white space?

Do You Know Your Likability Score?

According to Tim Sanders, author of *The Likeability Factor,* "You can win life's popularity contests." Sanders's research has shown that the more you are liked, the happier your life will be, and he coaches readers on four specific factors:

- friendliness: your ability to communicate liking and openness to others
- relevance: your capacity to connect with others' interests, wants, and needs
- empathy: your ability to recognize, acknowledge, and experience other people's feelings
- realness: the integrity that stands behind your likability and guarantees its authenticity.

In the world of personal branding, it's especially important to consider these factors in terms of your first impression. Your ability to demonstrate your likability begins with your first interaction with someone, and as we discussed that first interaction is likely to happen online.

Does your LinkedIn profile convey your likability?

PONDER THIS

Get your likability score by ranking yourself on a scale of 1-5 on the following questions:

- Are you interesting? Your profile needs to go beyond the facts— beyond your accomplishments and credentials. It needs to make you human and fascinating—making your audience want to know more. Your summary is the best place to demonstrate that you're interesting.
- Are you transparent? When you read your profile, does it seem vague, like you're hiding something?
- Are you generous? If your profile screams "Me, Me, Me," it will repel more than attract. Do you acknowledge others? Do you volunteer for organizations or offer to mentor others?
- Do you stand out? To get people to feel curious about you, your profile needs to be differentiated.

REMOTE CONTROL

It's easier to show how likable you are when you're chatting with someone at the watercooler or coffee station. There, you're more likely to ask about your colleague's recent trip to Italy than hold forth on the Six Sigma process you use in your work. To deliver the same likability, be deliberate about what you want to share about your personal life in your LinkedIn profile. Be human in a world of automated machines.

Combining Your Results

At CareerBlast, we created the LPTI—the LinkedIn Profile Type Indicator (Figure 5-1). When you combine the results from these two scales, you can determine if your profile makes you seem anemic, affable, accomplished, or admired.

Figure 5-1. LinkedIn Profile Type Indicator

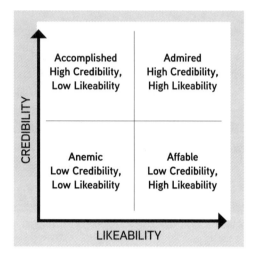

We have all heard it: "People want to work with people they know, like, and trust." Your LinkedIn profile needs to make people feel that they know you, then it needs build trust (that's the credibility piece) and get people to like you.

When you evaluate yourself in the two measures of credibility and likability, you will see where you show up in the four-box model: anemic, accomplished, affable, or admired.

Anemic

There's work to do. Your profile does little to build your credibility or help you connect with others. The great news is that, with a little effort, you can upgrade your profile and change the current perception. Reflect on your significant achievements and the things that people admire about you, as well as your audience's needs. Then refine your profile to include those key points.

Accomplished

Great start! You clearly communicate that you are skilled and have racked up numerous achievements. Now it's time to tweak your profile so that you are more approachable and immediately likable. To connect more deeply with others, share a bit more in your profile about who you are, what you're passionate about, and what you do outside of work.

Affable

Pretty good! Your LinkedIn profile exudes likability, making it easy for people to connect with you on a personal level. It's time to prove that you are not only likable, but also skilled and influential. To take your profile to the next level, add your workplace accomplishments and accolades from others. Show people who are checking you out that you have professional expertise, a honed point of view, and value to offer.

Admired

Bravo! You have built your LinkedIn profile thoughtfully and strategically. You deliver a powerful first impression. You not only communicate your accomplishments and accolades, but also connect deeply with others through your authenticity and transparency. You are both credible and likable, demonstrating that you are truly admirable.

To get your complete results, complete the complimentary LPTI quiz here: www.careerblast.tv/LPTI. It will reveal where you need to apply the most effort to your LinkedIn profile. We'll work on that profile in the next chapter. But before we do, here are two final, vital pointers:

Reorient your view of your profile. The best way to evaluate your profile is not to look at each of the LinkedIn elements in the order in which they're displayed. Instead, look at them from the perspective of the value they deliver for you (Table 5-1).

Table 5-1. LinkedIn Profile Components

COMPONENT	LINKEDIN CONTENT CATEGORIES	QUALITIES
The Big Three	Headline, Headshot, Summary/ About (this is your first impression)	Relevant, Magnetic, Compelling
Contact	Vanity URL, Contact Details, 3 Websites	Accessible, Visible
Validation	Endorsements, Recommendations, Experience, Education	Proven, Acknowledged
Other Elements	Articles and Activity, Accomplishments, Interests	Thorough, Professional, Well-Rounded, Involved

Don't annoy your connections. Before you start crafting your profile in chapter 6, do this one important thing. When you're updating your LinkedIn profile, it can annoy your contacts if they're alerted to every little change you make. Turn off "profile edit sharing." When you're on the homepage, go to Settings & Privacy (a menu option under "me") and under "Share job changes," choose "No." Then you can make all the changes you want over several sessions, and you won't alert your connections to each comma you add or word you change.

That's it. Now you're ready to translate the real you to the virtual you.

Summing Up

Chapter 5 was exclusively focused on LinkedIn—the most powerful online platform for delivering your first impression. You understand the important intersection of likability and credibility and are ready to turn this learning into action. That's what we'll discuss in chapter 6. You'll learn exactly what to do—and what not to do—to build a stellar LinkedIn profile, tapping the power of concepts that most LinkedIn users either skipped or never noticed. This will help you stand out.

CHAPTER 6

Build a Dazzling LinkedIn Profile

The Land of Digital Enchantment

Are you ready to build your brand in bits and bytes? We're going to upgrade enchanté and create the e-version—or e-nchanté.

In this chapter, I'll give you new insight into the most important elements of your LinkedIn profile, and I'll share everything you need to know for crafting a profile that is magnetic and compelling. My approach is designed with efficiency in mind, so I am not going to cover every single possible category of content—just the ones that are absolutely critical to your success.

Don't Confuse Complete With Compelling

LinkedIn gives you a percentage score for your profile. But that's not much of a metric. It just measures whether or not you have put something in every bucket. I have seen lots of lackluster profiles that scored 100 percent. Focus on the quality of your profile, not the quantity of your full buckets.

The most important components, and the ones we'll work on, are:

- The Big Three
- Contact
- Validation

The Big Three

Out of all the bells and whistles, there are three key elements of your profile that make a major difference when it comes to delivering your first impression and enticing people to want to know more. They are headshot, headline, and summary:

- **Headshot.** Your photo helps viewers connect a face with a name, and it makes you real in the often nebulous, impersonal world of the web.
- **Headline.** Think of this as the headline for an ad. Its job? To grab readers' attention.
- **Summary ("About").** This is the place that lets you come alive in the digital world. Surprisingly, many people on LinkedIn don't even fill out the summary (now labeled the "about") section.

I devote a lot of this chapter to these three important elements. If you don't get these right, you'll miss out on the true value of LinkedIn. Let's look at these vital ingredients individually:

Your Headshot

In a world where most people meet us online before they meet us in person, our audience wants to connect a face with a name. Your headshot makes you real in the weird world of the web. In addition, it helps you get noticed in LinkedIn.

 FUN FACT

"LinkedIn reports that users with a photo in their profile receive 21 times more profile views," according to Forbes contributor Marcia Layton Turner.

✔ **DO THIS,**
✘ **NOT THAT**

Do invest in a professional headshot. Have a photo taken specifically for this purpose. A sloppy, blurry snapshot makes you look like a sloppy, blurry amateur.	**Don't** use a selfie. All pictures are not created equal. Just having a picture in your profile is not enough to get people to want to engage with you.

Your headshot should add credibility to your profile—so make it professional. It's not just about having a photo. It's about having the right photo. Make your mug work for you on LinkedIn:

Fill the frame. Crop so that your face captures about 70-80 percent of the space. Your uploaded picture shows up in a circle, but the dimensions are 400 by 400 pixels. Remember that the shot will be used as a thumbnail when you participate in other features on LinkedIn, appearing far beyond the top of your listing. Whole body shots are too small to see—especially in sections like endorsements.

Face forward. Look into the eyes of the person who's checking you out. Don't look off-screen. This is your first impression!

Avoid the glum "I'm a serious professional" look. Ron Gutman's TED Talk, "The Hidden Power of Smiling," references a Penn State study that showed "when we smile, we not only appear more likeable and courteous, but we're actually perceived to be more competent." So smiling helps with both your LPTI Likability and Credibility measures!

Refer to chapter 7 for detailed advice on getting the best photo for LinkedIn and other social media.

Your Headline

Your headline's purpose is to get your target audience to want to read on. Yet most LinkedIn members think "headline = job title." If you don't write a headline, LinkedIn uses your current job title as a default, and that's a total bore.

When you limit your headline to your job title, like "Senior Manager, Risk and Compliance," you're making yourself a commodity—interchangeable with anyone else who shares that job title. To have your headline work for you, it should say what you do and entice people to learn more about your services. Don't make it all about you; make it about the people you serve. Tell viewers what you can do for them. It also needs to feature the keywords you want associated with your name. Use all 120 characters to solve these goals simultaneously. Here's the formula:

Be relevant + Be loyal + Be found + Be interesting
Job title + Company + Keywords + Zing

 BRAND HACK

Put your keywords in your headline. Make your headline serve as an online "magnet." If you want to be found in a LinkedIn search, pack your headline with the keywords for which you want to be known. Your headline is one of the most important profile elements in the search algorithm.

Here are some examples of effective headlines:
- #1 Relationship Author | Coaching & Consulting Leaders, Teams & Organizations on Improving Efficiency & Effectiveness
- Director of Business Development & Events Marketing— Building Lasting Impressions for Exhibitions & Events
- Talent Acquisition Leader, PMP—Attracting and Hiring the Best Talent in STEM and Project Management
- Human Resources Director, Compensation, Benefits & Talent Development Leader—Engaging Our People, Developing Leaders, Retaining Superstars

And one more major don't: If you're currently between formal jobs, don't use hollow headlines such as "Seeking my next big adventure" or

"Currently open to new opportunities." Those will work against you in a search (where are your keywords?) and the implication that you're not being productive right now makes you less attractive to some prospective employers. Recruiters favor employed passive candidates over those who are actively seeking employment. So focus on what you *are* doing. If you think you aren't doing anything, it's time to get moving on your side hustle or volunteer activities.

Your Summary (About)

After seeing your headshot and reading your headline, viewers of your profile check out your summary (titled "About" on the platform). This section piques their interest and makes them want to learn more.

Your summary is a story—your story. Make it an interesting and compelling narrative of you, what you're passionate about, and how you deliver value to your clients and colleagues. It needs to express the real you for those who meet you first online, so make a special effort to infuse it with your personality.

The old school of summary writing consisted of a series of credentials strung together in prose form. That won't cut it today. As your first impression, your LinkedIn summary has to do a lot more heavy lifting. Use it to paint a 3D portrait of who you are and tell people why they want to get to know you. It's time to take a look at your brand bio from chapter 3 and refine it for this medium.

 MINDSET
RESET

Conventional thinking says that the first line of your bio needs to show relevance. That's not the case with your LinkedIn summary. Your headline shows relevance. Don't waste the opportunity to connect deeply to viewers by repeating what you have already told them in your headline. Instead, entice them to get to know you.

✔ **DO THIS,**
✗ **NOT THAT**

Do be opinionated. Personal branding is not about trying to please everyone. Be courageous and show the world that you have a point of view.	**Don't** mimic. If you use your summary to fit in, you'll be lost in a sea of replicants, not the professional who shimmers.

Make the first three lines of your summary magnetic. When someone looks at your LinkedIn profile, only the first three lines of your summary are visible. Readers need to click "see more" to read the full story. If those first few lines aren't intriguing, viewers may not take action to see the rest.

"Because we tend to view our personal social media accounts as being 'personal,' there's a good chance that by viewing someone's profile, you'll get a glimpse into their personality beyond the resume," says DeeAnn Sims, founder of marketing firm SPBX.

Your summary has the most potential to connect you emotionally with viewers of your profile. It can attract and it can repel. So getting your summary right is essential. To get you started, see Figure 6-1 for six helpful tips.

Tool 6-1. Six Ways to Begin Your Summary With a Bang!

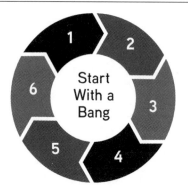

Start With a Bang

1. Purpose
2. Promise
3. Punctuated List
4. Point in Time
5. Passion
6. Provocative Phrase

I have read thousands of LinkedIn summaries and realized that the best ones start in one of these six ways. Here are examples of those critical first few lines in each of the six categories. This will give you a feel for how it works. Next, I've shared examples of some of the most authentic, differentiated, and compelling summaries I have read (and I have read a *lot* of summaries).

1. Purpose

People are my business. I believe it's more important to be interested than interesting, and it's my mission to really get to know each person I meet and to build deep, trust-based relationships with them. This is true in my personal life and in my role of account manager for web development services.

2. Promise

I accelerate your business performance through the power of people. It's my mission to find the most qualified, interesting, and engaged professionals on earth and help you bring them onto your team. How do I do it? I combine my inquisitive nature with my power networking and research skills to uncover exceptional, hidden talent.

3. Punctuated List

Lifelong learner. Loyal corporate citizen with an entrepreneurial spirit. Curious questioner of "all things tech." My job title is product researcher, but I act as if I'm an owner. In that capacity, I'm committed to innovating (especially through technology) and to making decisions that meet the strategic needs of our product team.

4. Point in Time

I was working at a startup in Silicon Valley when a member of my team told me about a new company that was combining artificial intelligence with data analytics to deliver insights and predict customer actions. I became intrigued by value this would provide to our sales team.

(This is also the style I chose for my LinkedIn Summary: www.linkedin .com/in/williamarruda.)

5. Passion

Five. Seven. Eighty-Three. Those are the number of languages I speak, countries I have lived in, and major cities I've visited—in that order. When you grow up the daughter of a diplomat, it's easy to be a citizen of the world. My itinerant lifestyle and passion for travel and diverse cultures inspired me to pursue a career in international relations. Now, as the head of . . .

6. Provocative Phrase

My business is going downhill—fast. I'm an outdoor enthusiast, former professional skier, and the founder of the Ski Academy. Skiing can be the antidote to life's constant stressors. I'm committed to building invigorating experiences that help people . . .

Select Your Sizzling Start

Take a look at the content you prepared in chapter 3 and determine which of the six sizzling starts described here will be best for you. Then, work on the first few lines of your summary. They're like the wall a swimmer pushes against to fuel the next lap. Getting them right gives you the momentum you need to craft the rest of your summary—the most-read version of your bio.

After you have mastered your kickoff, weave together content from the six content buckets you filled in chapter 3, or just edit the long-play version of your bio that you wrote in that chapter. And save some of your 2,000 characters for two really important elements that you'll use just in your LinkedIn profile:

- AKA/common misspellings
- specialties.

Common Misspellings

Don't assume others know how you spell your name or know that you've changed your name. Include all known misspellings, previous names, nicknames, and aliases in your summary. That way, even if people don't know the correct spelling of your name or the fact that you changed your name or go by a nickname, they'll still end up at your profile. In addition to focusing on your target audience, don't forget one very important reader of your profile: Google's search algorithm.

Specialties

Repeat your keywords as often as possible in your profile. One easy way to do that is to take the words you want to associate yourself with and list them in order of importance at the bottom of your summary. Remember to include the keywords related to where you want to be next. Although personal branding is grounded in authenticity, there's an important aspirational element. Make yourself relevant for what's next.

Congrats, You Made It

That's it! When you enhance those elements, you take your profile from average to awesome, OK to OMG, ow to wow. And you establish a powerful first impression with those who are checking you out.

When you're happy with your draft summary, test it with these two methods: Get feedback and ask yourself questions.

Get Feedback

Identify at least three trusted people to provide honest feedback:
- a member of your target audience
- a mentor, coach, or trusted advisor who wants you to succeed
- a personal friend or family member who knows you well.

Ask Yourself Questions

Use the questions from the following Ponder This as your guide.

 PONDER THIS

Is my summary stellar? Read your profile—paying close attention to what you read.

- Do the first couple of sentences make me want to read more?
- Is it authentic—a real portrayal of who I am?
- Does it help me stand out from my peers—others who seek to achieve what I'm looking to achieve?
- Is it relevant—addressing the needs of the people I'm trying to attract?
- Does it have personality—connecting people with my style?
- Is it clear to the reader how I add value—going beyond a listing of accomplishments?
- Is it compelling—with interesting or unexpected facts and details that make the reader want to get to know more?
- Is it pleasing to look at? Did I create enough white space to break up the paragraphs? Did I write good subheadlines for different content blocks?
- Are the grammar and punctuation perfect?
- Does it include all the keywords for which I want to be known? This is extremely important in both creating relevance and making sure you are found in a search.
- Did I include some validation (things like "People say I'm . . . " or a quote from a great evaluation, or mention of an award for my work)?

Finalize your summary, refining it based on the feedback you received and the edits your questioning spawns. Then upload the final version to your profile and bask in the wonderful comments you receive from your LinkedIn connections.

Take a look at Brandi's summary. It's drawn from the results of her exercises in chapter 3, and it uses Start With a Bang approaches 4 and 6 (point in time and provocative phrase).

BRANDI
BRAINSTORMS

When I was ten years old, I persuaded my dad to let me eat a cricket. He was on a business trip in Thailand (getting him to take me along was another feat of persuasion). He made his pitch: If I didn't like my snack of fried crickets, he didn't want to waste time and money for me to order something else. And I made my pitch: What was the point of traveling if I was just going to eat the same stuff we had at home?

I ended up loving everything that street vendor cooked, and the experience opened the door to my lifelong passion for diving deep into cultures that are new to me while building relationships based on mutual respect and unabashed curiosity.

To this day, my nickname in the industry is The Persuader, and that success is directly tied to my ability to work past differences to uncover innovative marketing opportunities. My approach has led to global advertising campaigns that reeled in $500,000 in new business while reducing our clients' media spend, and my teams stick with me for the long haul—maybe because I make it a priority to continually dream up new destinations for their creativity.

Contact

Make it easy for people to connect with you and learn more about you.

First, edit your vanity URL so it reads: linkedin.com/in/yourname. Then, add the ways you'd like people to contact you (email address, phone number, Twitter handle, and so on). Lastly, use the three website links to point to other places that help you expand or reinforce your story. You can point to things like:

- your company website (show that you're loyal to your employer) or to the section of the company website that talks about what you do
- YouTube videos you're featured in
- articles you have written or are quoted in
- other examples of work you have done
- your social media accounts.

Validation

When it comes to branding yourself online, you need to tell people what makes you exceptional, and you need to prove what you say about yourself with input from others. Validate what you say in your summary with external proof in four areas:

- experience
- education
- endorsements
- recommendations.

Experience

Your experience blocks allow you to provide more details about what you wrote in your summary. Each block allows for a 2,000-character description. For each experience block, remember to choose the company you worked for from LinkedIn's list so the company logo shows up.

✔ DO THIS,
✘ NOT THAT

Do be clear about the things you want to be known for today and what will make yourself relevant for tomorrow. Make sure your profile screams those things.	**Don't** include details of every job you've had. Omit (or combine under a heading like "previous experience") your early jobs that don't offer insights to how you deliver value today.

Education

List all your education, including continuing education you've completed since graduation. Choosing your school from the LinkedIn list is one more way to add proof (and your school's logo) to your profile.

Endorsements

Let's face it. Endorsements seem silly. Yet we make judgments about people based on the skills for which they were endorsed, and LinkedIn showcases those skills in a way that delivers tremendous visual impact. Only the three skills with the most endorsements show up when someone looks at your profile. Viewers need to click "show more" to see the rest of your skills, but it's critical that you emphasize the three most important skills that you want people to associate with you.

 BRAND HACK

Reorder your skills. Most people don't know it, but LinkedIn allows you to reorder your skills so they appear in order of importance to you— regardless of how many endorsements you have received for them. Pick the ones that bolster your personal brand and will help you advance your career and put those in the top three spots. Then ask for endorsements of those skills. Once you reach 99 endorsements or more, LinkedIn doesn't show the actual number.

Be ungrateful. By that I mean be willing to delete endorsements for skills that just muddy the waters. Personal branding requires focus and potency.

Recommendations

When others praise you, they provide the credibility that bolsters your brand. LinkedIn's recommendations feature helps you prove what you say about yourself in your profile. The most powerful recommendations meet as many of these criteria as possible. A recommendation is helpful based on:

- **What it says.** A useful recommendation is more than just glowing words. Those words should reinforce how you want to be known—highlighting proof of what makes you great.

- **Who says it.** Testimonials that come from people who are revered in your community or who have a senior or respected job title have more weight.
- **Where the recommender works.** When your recommender comes from a well-known, respected brand, some of that brand value rubs off on you in terms of brand association.

How do you get recommendations? First, make sure the person whose recommendation you seek is one of your LinkedIn connections.

✔ DO THIS,
✘ NOT THAT

Do use your personal or work email for your recommendation request. It will be more likely that you'll get a response, and it will give you the opportunity to influence what it says.	**Don't** request a LinkedIn recommendation from within LinkedIn until you have asked your recommender if it's OK to send a request through LinkedIn. Busy people often ignore messages that come from LinkedIn.

To make your recommendation reinforce what you want people to associate with you, when you make your email request, offer reminders of how you have provided value to the recommender, or even provide a basic draft of the recommendation, with a note like this:

I know you're extremely busy, so I'd be happy to send you an outline you can edit (or of course throw away), or even a draft, if that would make it easier for you.

Then, in your draft, highlight the attributes that will be most helpful to bolstering your brand. Of course, you need to have demonstrated those attributes!

Even if they choose to ignore what you have sent, you have likely influenced what they're thinking as they prepare to write their recommendation.

Completing Your Profile

You don't need me or this book to help you complete your profile, filling out the remaining sections on specifics ranging from publications to volunteer work. The LinkedIn "help" feature will give you answers to any questions related to those straightforward elements. Because they're so easy to complete, it's tempting to spend a lot of time on those sections. Resist the urge. Spend your time and energy on honing the crucial components covered in-depth in this chapter.

✔ **DO THIS,**
✘ **NOT THAT**

Do know the difference between complete and compelling. Focus less on filling in every box and more on making what you put in the boxes significant.	**Don't** use LinkedIn's profile metric of completeness as a measure of how powerful your profile is.

Beyond LinkedIn

Before we move from words to pictures in the next section, there's one more thing to do: Transfer what you learned about your digital first impression and LinkedIn to other social media that you plan to use for building your brand.

There are several tools that I think are especially valuable to most career-minded professionals: Twitter, YouTube, SlideShare, Instagram, and Facebook. Of course, there are dozens of other potential platforms to check out. Ultimately, you should choose the ones that will help you express your message to the people who count. We'll talk more about these tools in part 4, but for now, I want to focus on creating a powerful first impression with social media beyond LinkedIn. Here's what you need to do:

1. **Claim your vanity URL.** For the social media tools you'd like to use but still haven't set up an account for (and for the tools that you think you might want to use sometime in the future) go to

Knowem.com and put your name in the search box. It will reveal which sites still have your name available.

2. **Set up your profile.**

3. **Add your headshot and bio**—make them relevant to the style and type of platform. For example, you might use your most professional headshot for LinkedIn, but use a more casual one on Instagram or Facebook. See Table 6-1 for specs.

Table 6-1. Social Media Bio/Photo Specs

PLATFORM	BIO CHARACTER LIMIT	PHOTO DIMENSIONS
Twitter	160	400 x 400 pixels, 2MB
SlideShare (Slideshare.net)	700	96 x 96 pixels, 500KB
YouTube	980 (called channel description)	800 x 800 pixels
Instagram	150	110 x 110 pixels
Facebook	100 (called intro)	At least 180 x 180 pixels

As for Twitter, even if you think tweeting is more appropriate for Justin Bieber than for you, it's a valuable tool for increasing your visibility on the web—even if you don't have any followers yet (more on that in part 4).

Writing your Twitter bio is an excellent branding exercise because it makes you distill your brand into just 160 characters. And because it's Twitter, it gives you an opportunity to be playful with your prose. The next Ponder This shares my process for gathering the raw content to craft it.

 PONDER THIS

What should I put in my Twitter bio?

- Who are the people I am looking to influence on this channel and what about me is interesting and relevant to them?
- What are three things I want them to know about me?

- What's my brand differentiation or secret sauce?
- What am I passionate about?
- What can I say that will validate my self-proclamations?

BRANDI BRAINSTORMS

Brandi's answers to those questions:

- I want to land new clients for our global marketing agency . . . and the right clients: highly profitable, preferably tech sector, and other growth industries. And I'm ready to become a VP here, where I can be more influential. My international expertise is relevant and interesting.
- I'm curious, creative, and a collaborator.
- I'm The Persuader.
- Helping people understand that differences make humanity stronger. They help us fill in each other's gaps. There's too much divisiveness in the world. I like working in global marketing because I see myself as an ambassador. My messages build bridges.
- My campaigns work. I have plenty of data to show that my strategies turn up the volume and stoke sales.

Brandi's Twitter bio:

I'm an award-winning global marketer who climbs mountains, persuades naysayers, and inspires game-changing collaborations. Being human is a team sport.

And here's my Twitter bio—coming in at 155 characters:

CEO-Chief Encouragement Officer. Personal branding expert. Motivational speaker. Bestselling author. Aesthete. Urbanist. Twizzler addict. Eternal optimist.

Summing Up

Feeling accomplished? In chapter 6, you focused your branding activities on delivering a powerful digital first impression—one that's aligned with your real-world brand. You have a LinkedIn profile that will introduce you to your brand community—a profile that will be the envy of your peers.

Phew! Now, we're going to take a little break from creating the text you use to describe yourself. In chapter 7, we'll turn our attention from words to pictures, and we'll discuss how to be real through vivid visuals in the nebulous and often confusing world of the web. So get ready to have some fun with photos.

Part 3
Visual You

"Humans are incredibly visual and powerful. Moving images help us find meaning [and] help capture and contextualize the world around us."
—Dan Patterson, Digital Platform Manager for ABC Radio

PART 3

Visual You

With the real-to-virtual translation process behind you, it's time to think about amping up the appeal of your communications. In this part of the book, we'll talk about using images, video, color, and other techniques to make your communications more persuasive and alluring. Specifically, we're going to discuss:

- **pictures:** how your headshot and other images can make you real and connect you more deeply with your community online
- **packaging:** how to create the right wrapper for your brand
- **video:** how to use the most powerful communications vehicle there is—next to being there in person, of course.

When you've applied what you learn in part 3 to the virtual you that was developed in part 2, you'll have what you need to build your community and bolster your brand; you'll then be ready to boost your success, which we'll cover in part 4.

CHAPTER 7

Leverage the Power of Pictures

Picture This

a b c d e f g h i j k l m n o p q r s t u v w x y z

That's all you have when you are communicating with words alone. Let's face it: Text can be boring.

Email is mostly annoying—and overwhelming, right?

IM + txting r perhaps the lowest frms of xpression 2day. They strip all the meaning and nuance from communication.

And emojis and emoticons don't cut it, regardless of how many you use to adorn your messages :)

The most powerful form of communication is face-to-face conversation. But in a world that's becoming more and more virtual, in-person communication is less and less feasible.

To get your digital brand seen, heard, understood, and embraced, a rich media presence is essential. Groundbreaking research by communication scholars W. Howard Levie and Richard Lentz, released in various scholarly publications including *Educational Communications* and *Technology Journal*, underscored the deep cognitive and emotional impact of visuals on us.

Cognitively, images speed up and expand our level of communication and increase comprehension, recollection, and retention. Emotionally, visuals engage our imagination and heighten our creative thinking by stimulating other areas of our brain, which translates into deeper and more accurate understanding.

When it comes to helping people get to know you in the digital world, pictures and videos are potent communications vehicles. They help you convey your humanity, your message, and your style.

In this chapter, we'll focus on pictures, specifically photography, and the photo elements that you will use to create your own digital design and brand. Then, in chapter 8, I'll use those concepts to help you define the packaging for your brand. In chapter 9, we'll put it all together for the ultimate visuals, turning our attention to moving pictures.

Before we jump into the exciting world of images, let's adopt the right mindset.

 MINDSET RESET

In the past, your company invested time, money, and other resources in your career advancement. Those days are over. You are now the CEO of You, Inc., and you need to allocate resources for these responsibilities. If you find yourself wanting to skimp on your visuals (can't we just take a quick selfie with our phone and call it a headshot?), ask yourself if you'd want to work for a CEO who skimped on the most visible elements of her brand. A professional headshot and maybe even a graphic design consultant are not expenses; they're investments that pay dividends.

You need to be willing (read "excited") to invest financially in the outcome of your career, not only in visuals. There are three areas you need to devote funds to:

- branded personal marketing materials (headshot, packaging, portfolios)

- branded learning—professional development and training in your key service areas, to keep the saw sharp
- branded environment, from your office (especially when it's the backdrop for videoconferencing) to the cafés you choose for meeting with clients and doing off-site brainstorming.

Pictures of You

Let's start with pictures. It's time to start investing in art. Specifically, pictures—of you.

Put Your Best Face Forward

Your headshot makes you real in the virtual world—the weird and nebulous place that's often met with incredulity. People are more likely to believe what you say about yourself or the content you share if there's a photograph of you to make it real. My clients tell me they steer clear of LinkedIn profiles without headshots. LinkedIn's research backs this up: "Profiles with professional headshots get up to 21 times more views" (Callahan 2018).

BRAND HACK

Get a series of pics. When you set up a session with a photographer, plan to have a series of different headshots with different wardrobes. You will be using your headshot in different social media and want to make sure you have the right image for each of the different scenarios. Different backdrops can also help increase the variety while demonstrating your versatility.

Not All Headshots Are Created Equal

Some people don't take it seriously when they upload headshots to their social media profiles. They look through their photos on their iPhone or laptop, pick one, and that's it. I have seen numerous headshots that actually make me want to avoid the person rather than create a connection with them. To protect the guilty, I won't share those names here. What I will share is exactly what you need to be thinking about so your headshot can make you real—and really likable—to those who are checking you out online.

✔ **DO THIS,**
✘ **NOT THAT**

Do invest in a professional photographer. Check out their work to make sure you like the style and end results.	**Don't** use a photo you have on your phone or the picture your partner took of you at last year's family outing.

The best headshots are:

About You!

- Don't use images featuring multiple people. I think it's great that you enjoy collaborating or that you adore your kids, but when it comes to your professional headshot, it needs to be about you.
- Don't use a logo in place of your face. As proud as you are of your company, using the logo takes the humanity out of message. Save the logo for your company communications, and make your mug front and center.
- Don't use images where you've cropped others out of the frame; it's just plain weird to see part of your arm or someone else's hair in your headshot.

Professional

- Don't use selfies—save them for Instagram or Snapchat.
- Use photos that were taken for the purpose of conveying your professional value.
- Wear clothes that help you exude your brand and are relevant to the people you're looking to influence.

Pervasive

- Don't leave the headshot field blank in any of your social media profiles—this makes you less real and more dubious in the virtual world.
- Use different photos on different sites to be relevant for the various platforms and show the range of your personality. When someone does a Google image search on you, they should see a series of subtly different headshots—not one headshot repeated 10 times!

Current

- Don't use a photo that was taken a decade ago, even if it is your favorite.
- Make sure if someone is meeting you for the first time after seeing your picture on the web, they can pick you out in a crowded Starbucks.

Prepare for Your Headshot

Because of the work I do with companies, helping their people build stellar LinkedIn profiles, I have looked at a lot of headshots—thousands. Now that you're convinced of the need for professional photos, here's what you need to do to master that first visual impression.

Face forward. This allows you to look into the eyes of those checking you out online. Avoid side-profiles and shadowy shots.

"A smile is the universal welcome."
—Max Eastman

Smile. We all know how important it is to greet everyone you meet with a smile. Well, smiling works in the two-dimensional world of pictures, too. In an article in Psychology Today, Wendy Patrick says, "Your photo selection can quickly define your online desirability—or lack thereof. Even if you are incredibly handsome, a straight-faced photo might look more like a mug shot than a glamour shot."

BRAND HACK

Close your eyes. This brand hack comes from Clare Jones, Founder of Clare Jones London. "Close your eyes a couple of seconds before you know the picture will be taken, then open them and slowly draw up the corners of your mouth. This can help to offset nerves and reset your state."

Choose your background. It's part of the big picture. Whether you choose a simple or elaborate background image for your headshot, it must truly exude your personal brand. You can choose a white background if you're all about clarity, or use your brand color (check out chapter 8 for more information on how to choose the color that's perfect for you). If you don't use a plain background, make sure that what you choose is not so busy that it distracts the viewer.

Perfect Your Photo

Use Photox. Photox is a lot less painful than Botox, and it lasts a lot longer. Photox is my word for minor photo retouching. Just don't go overboard. It's OK if you remove the shine from your face and edit out an errant hair—just make sure the photo still looks like you.

Crop it. Remember, unlike the headshots of models or actors that end up as 8x10 glossies, the final version of your headshot will be more like the size of a postage stamp—and for most social profiles it will appear in a square or a circle. It will end up online as part of a social media profile, often being viewed on a small mobile screen. That means you should focus on the "head" part of your headshot. Crop your image so about 75 percent of the real estate is your face. This will help you connect more deeply with those who are checking you out. Avoid full body shots because it will be that much harder to connect with you—especially on phones.

Upload Your Photo

Your photos have value only if people see them. So upload photos to:

- All your social media sites—choosing the right one for the tone and audience.
- Your email signature. If your company doesn't allow you to do this, add it to your personal email signature in Gmail or Apple mail, for example.
- Your personal website, if you have one.

))) REMOTE
CONTROL

Your headshot plays an even more important role if you're not co-located with your colleagues. Add your headshot to the bottom of your email and in all online places where you show up, including your profiles. Also, make sure you add your photo everywhere possible on each of your company's communications tools, including the intranet (Spark, Jive), on video conferencing platforms (Zoom, Skype, Join.me), and in all the other appropriate places. That way, even if you aren't physically in the office, people nonetheless see your smiling face all day long in all your communications.

BRAND
HACK

Name your pics YOURNAME.JPG. Before uploading your photos to various websites and social media platforms, be sure to name the files yourname.jpg. Although some sites will change the name of the photo you upload, in many cases, the file name of your picture sticks. When you label your photo with your name, two great things happen: 1) It will likely appear on page one of a Google search on your name (thanks to universal search), and 2) it will show up when someone does a Google image search on your name.

Here are some headshots I think really capture the essence of their subject (Figure 7-1).

Figure 7-1. Example Headshots

Images Beyond Your Headshot

There are hundreds of ways to use images to build your brand and numerous social media platforms that enable it—too many to talk about here. What I want to share are three of what I believe are the most powerful ways to use visuals to get your message to the people who need to know you:

- SlideShare
- infographics
- Instagram.

SlideShare

If you create presentations as part of what you do, or prefer creating content in PowerPoint, Keynote, or Google Slides instead of using plain documents, SlideShare is for you. SlideShare is a platform for housing and sharing slide presentations and other multimedia. LinkedIn purchased SlideShare in 2012 and since then has created a strong integration between the two platforms. SlideShare is a powerful tool for expressing your thought leadership and repurposing content that you develop for your work and your professional affiliations.

 FUN FACT

> According to John Medina in his book *Brain Rules: 12 Principles for Surviving and Thriving at Work, Home, and School*, when people hear information, they're likely to remember only 10 percent of it three days later. However, if a relevant image is paired with that same information, they retain 65 percent of the information three days later.

Of course, you cannot share presentations that you develop for your employer containing confidential information or references to proprietary information from clients. But if you deliver a presentation to your local professional association or teach a lunch and learn (and have your company's permission to share the content), you have instant material to use to expand your brand visibility way beyond the number of people in the room who participated in your presentation. According to the SlideShare website, over 80 percent of SlideShare's 80 million visitors come through targeted search. This will allow you to demonstrate your brand value to a wide community of people who search for topics related to your expertise.

When you publish the PDF of a slide presentation on SlideShare, you can instantly make it available to your connections and groups at LinkedIn, and you can add it to your LinkedIn profile in the summary or experience sections. I'll share some other really cool features about Slide-Share in chapter 12.

Infographics

When you're looking to build your thought leadership, infographics are powerful. Why? The combination of words and associated images makes them attractive. Eye-tracking studies show online readers pay close attention to information-carrying images. In fact, when the images are relevant, readers spend more time looking at the images than they do reading text on the page. And they're more likely to share them, too. According to Hubspot, "visual assets are the single biggest content contributor" on social media.

Creating infographics also gives you an opportunity to organize your thought leadership into easy-to-digest and shareable chunks. If what you do has a process or system, it's ideal to use an infographic to explain it. Infographics are also helpful when you're delivering a presentation. They can show the overall structure of your content and remind people how the current topic you're discussing fits into the bigger picture. You can leave participants with a handout of the infographic as a valuable takeaway. And when you post your infographics online, you amp up visibility. Infographics can also increase web traffic by up to 12 percent (Demand Gen Report 2014).

To create infographics, you can use tools like Venngage, Visme, or Snappa. Or, if it's a really important infographic—one that will have a long shelf life and will be good for helping you stand out—you can find and hire a designer at visual.ly, UpWork, or Remote.com.

Posting infographics is easy. Although there are sites that focus specifically on infographics (like graphs.net and Infographicsshowcase.com), most of them charge for you to post your work. You can post your infographics to any of the visual social media sites where your target audience lives—not only to SlideShare but also Instagram, Pinterest, and Facebook. See Figure 7-2 for an example infographic that describes the content of this book.

Figure 7-2. Example Infographic

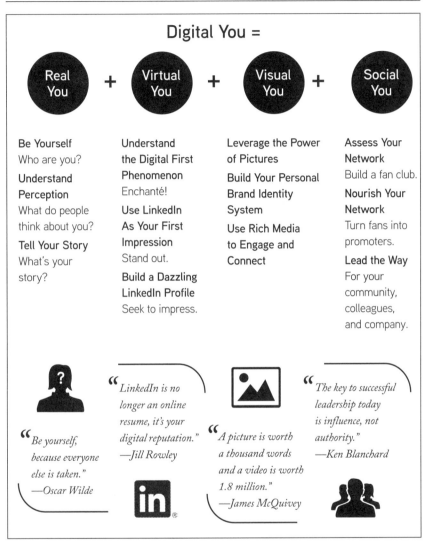

Digital You =

Real You + **Virtual You** + **Visual You** + **Social You**

Be Yourself	**Understand the Digital First Phenomenon**	**Leverage the Power of Pictures**	**Assess Your Network**
Who are you?	Enchanté!	**Build Your Personal Brand Identity System**	Build a fan club.
Understand Perception	**Use LinkedIn As Your First Impression**	**Use Rich Media to Engage and Connect**	**Nourish Your Network**
What do people think about you?	Stand out.		Turn fans into promoters.
Tell Your Story	**Build a Dazzling LinkedIn Profile**		**Lead the Way**
What's your story?	Seek to impress.		For your community, colleagues, and company.

"Be yourself, because everyone else is taken." —Oscar Wilde

"LinkedIn is no longer an online resume, it's your digital reputation." —Jill Rowley

"A picture is worth a thousand words and a video is worth 1.8 million." —James McQuivey

"The key to successful leadership today is influence, not authority." —Ken Blanchard

BRANDI BRAINSTORMS

Infographics are it. They provide me with an opportunity to be creative and they can be quite persuasive. One of the ways I persuade is with data. I'll design infographics of client campaigns, including results data and analysis. And to show the power of infographics as a tool for persuasion, I'll print them out and post them on my office wall—creating a colorful wallpaper that showcases my team's efforts and successes.

Instagram

Publishing presentations to SlideShare and creating infographics are most valuable when you're looking to combine text and images. If your focus is more on images and less on text, Instagram might be the best vehicle for you. There are more than 500 million Instagram users active every day.

Pictures are powerful—that includes pics of you and pictures that allow you to express your brand and engage your audience. But remember, you need to make it easy for people to find your images. That means you need to use all relevant hashtags—up to the Instagram limit of 30. New York City–based family and divorce attorney–mediator Chris Sorensen, whose Instagram handle is riversidewanderernyc said, "When I started adding 30 relevant hashtags to the pics I take on my walks to and from my Columbus Circle office, I experienced a significant increase in views and followers."

Summing Up

With your confident smile and mug prominently displayed online and some ideas for how to use pictures to engage your audience, it's time to talk about the aura that surrounds your brand—specifically, your personal brand identity system (PBID). In chapter 8, you'll learn how to craft an attractive PBID that's congruent with your brand, drawing on the intensive process you've completed that helped you unearth the real you. We'll discuss in detail all the visual elements that combine to form the branded wrapper for your communications.

CHAPTER 8

Build Your Personal Brand Identity System

Design the Package

When I was living in Europe, I was on a BBC reality TV show pilot called *Nice Package.* Now before your mind wanders into X-rated territory, *Nice Package* referred to everything that surrounds someone—in the case of this reality show, someone you want to date. In this pilot for the series, a young single woman got to check out everything about three potential dates— everything, that is, except the guy himself. Together, we rummaged through the guys' apartments, talked to their friends, drove in their cars, visited their favorite pubs, and so forth. I was the guest personal branding expert for the show and was tasked with helping her make sense of the brand environments of these three potential suitors.

Being on this show reinforced for me how much you can learn about someone from the things that (and people who) surround them. So when it comes to branding, it's important to align everything that surrounds you with who you are and how you want to be known. When you do, you bolster your brand. When your surroundings are not consistent with who you are, you create confusion and dilute your brand. We talked about the external perceptions element—what people think about you—in chapter 2. And we'll talk about your brand community in chapter 10—the people who surround your brand. In this chapter, we are going to talk about the packaging that helps deliver your brand to those audiences.

Specifically, we're going to discuss your personal brand identity (PBID)— it's the all-important container for digital brand you.

Let's start with a mindset reset.

 **MINDSET
RESET**

Packaging is not just for cereal boxes and corporations. Just as companies hire top designers to create high-quality, consistent packaging elements, you too should see your "packaging" as an investment in your career, not an expense that you'll never recapture. Don't skimp on time or money when it comes to standing out from your peers.

First, we'll talk about the individual elements of your PBID. Then, we'll focus on applying your brand identity to your digital brand communications.

Your PBID is the visual vernacular for your brand. And thanks to the move to digital, it includes all rich-media elements that help you reinforce your personal brand attributes. This rich-media design system includes the visuals, sound, motion, and other elements you will use consistently as the wrapper to all your communications. This wrapper helps to reinforce your brand attributes and create recognition. Your PBID is made up of three elements: visual, audio, and video.

The visual elements include:

- color
- font
- textures
- images.

The audio elements include:

- scripts
- intro tracks
- microphones.

We'll talk about video elements in chapter 9.

Now, you might be thinking: I don't need a PBID. I work for a company and am planning on working for The Man (or The Ma'am) for the rest of my career. Well, that's all great, but remember the career trends I discussed at the beginning of this book:

- You will likely change roles frequently throughout your career, even if you manage to stay at the same company for the long haul.
- Your company may not be around for as long as you'll be working.
- Searching for a job is much harder work than having your ideal job find you.
- Digital branding requires that you convey a consistent message and exude a consistent digital personality.

And besides, you'll be building a community of people (we'll talk about that in part 4) who need to see you as a polished expert and thought leader; that requires you use a consistent visual system for creating recognition and memorability.

Of course, when you're communicating on behalf of your company, you must follow their brand identity guidelines, but for all of your communications, your PBID is an essential element.

Choosing Your Visual Elements

Now let's create your own language—the visual vocabulary of your brand.

Brand Color

Color is the most important of all of the visual elements of your PBID. That's because color exudes brand attributes, evokes emotion, and creates recognition and memorability. NYU professor Adam Alter, who wrote *Drunk Tank Pink*, puts it like this: "Color sells, it persuades, it cajoles."

Here's a quick quiz:

Take a look at the brands in the left column in this table, and identify their brand color (Table 8-1).

Table 8-1. Name That Brand Color

BRAND	COLOR?
Avis	
Breast cancer research	
IBM	
McDonald's	
Harley Davidson	
Cadbury	
Google	

If you guessed red, pink, blue, yellow, orange, purple, and red/yellow/ green/blue (in that order)—you score an A! You also proved my point about the fact that color can communicate a consistent brand identity.

Building Brand Hue

Color can be extremely powerful—especially on the web, or in all those situations that require you to convey your brand without the benefit of being there in person. When you develop a strategy for using color on all your communications and apply it consistently, you'll become memorable, and you'll stand out from others who do what you do.

When I say apply color to all your communications, I suggest you select one color and use it consistently. Resist the temptation to use all 64 colors in a box of Crayola crayons. Sure, in our quiz above you may have guessed the four colors of the Google brand, but the revenue of their parent company, Alphabet, was about $140 billion in their fiscal year 2018. So they likely have a lot more money for making their brand colors visible and recognized. Plus, they've now aligned themselves with the multicolor approach, so that option is off the table for you. Your assignment is to choose the single best color for your brand.

✔ DO THIS,
✘ NOT THAT

Do choose the color that best represents your personality.	**Don't** choose your favorite color—unless it also expresses your brand.

Every color exudes certain personality characteristics. For example, yellow says optimism while blue connotes trust. Check out this video to help you identify the perfect brand color to reinforce your personality: http://360rea.ch/YourBrandColor. The video shows you what each of the six primary and secondary colors expresses.

After you watch the video, select the color that best represents your brand. You may want to go back to part 1 of this book to remind yourself of the most important elements of your brand—the brand attributes that are authentic, differentiating, and compelling to your target audience. Your color could be the one that exudes the largest number of brand attributes that describe you, or it could be the color that expresses that one word that is so important to who you are and how you want to be known.

Once you identify the best color for your personal brand, select the specific tint or shade you'd like to use. The best site to help with this is Pantone Colours. Once you know the Pantone Matching System (PMS) color, you can determine the HEX value. PMS color is for printed materials, whereas HEX is used for digital applications. You can convert your PMS to HEX easily here: https://360rea.ch/ConvertColor.

And since you are going to be using your brand color on the web, I suggest choosing one of the web-safe colors—the closest to the color you selected using the Pantone system. There are 216 web-safe colors. They're called web safe because they display consistently on various hardware environments, operating systems, and web browsers. You can find a web-safe color resource here: https://websafecolors.info/color-chart.

Now if all this seems way too "designer" to you, you can always hire a designer inexpensively (remember, it's an investment!) who will be able to manage all this for you. Upwork.com is a great resource for finding a graphic designer.

Once you have your brand color, whenever you need to create visual communications, you can apply it consistently. For example, the primary brand color I have chosen for myself is yellow, which exudes optimism and positivity.

Ways to Use Color

Here are some ideas for ways to use color for brand differentiation and memorability:

- Apply it to your personal website, blog, or vlog if you have one.
- Create your own stationery system—letterhead, business cards, envelopes, and so on featuring your signature color in those real-world communications.
- Develop PowerPoint/Word or Keynote/Pages templates that feature your brand color.
- Create branded thank-you notes to acknowledge others.
- Add it to your Twitter background.
- Use it in your YouTube channel. YouTube lets you choose the color of your channel or completely customize it.
- Update your Facebook page with your signature color.
- Make it the background color for your headshot or avatar that you post alongside your online profiles (in LinkedIn and other social media).

- Use it in your videos, as a background color and for the intro and outro. Or, do what IBM does in their TV ads and use the letterbox style, which features a band of color above and below the video.
- Use it as a screen saver as a reminder of your brand color.
- Include a dose of color in your email signature in all correspondence with your contacts.

Understanding Brand Fonts

Using fonts consistently can help people recognize communications as coming from you. There are two primary types of fonts—serif fonts (they're the ones with the little tails) and sans serif, without the tails ("sans" means "without" in French). Times New Roman and Georgia are examples of serif fonts. Serif fonts have a long history. They've been around since the Roman Empire. According to Sarah Hyndman, founder of the Type Tasting studio, in an interview published on Moo.com, "Type is our voice, so the typeface you use very much reflects your personality. It works as a first impression, in a very similar way to our clothes. For example, if I set something in a serif typeface, it's the equivalent of me wearing my glasses—it's been shown that people interpret words in serif as well researched and more intellectual."

Sans serif fonts are newer and more modern. Common ones include Helvetica and Verdana. Sarah advises that you use your typeface to tell the story you want to tell. "Your branding should reflect your personality or attitude—serious and well informed, open and modern, or relaxed and casual. For example, the Cooper Black font says '70s nostalgia and sunshine,' while Benguiat says '80s authentic' (think *Stranger Things*). Or you can use it to communicate with a particular tribe, using typefaces and tone of voice to connect with your target audience."

If your brand is more traditional, serious, or formal, you might want to choose a serif font. If you're going for a more modern and innovative feel, sans serif might be right. Whichever you choose as your primary font, use it consistently in your documents, PowerPoint presentations, infographics, and other materials.

Applying Textures

I'm a big fan of creating and using consistent textures. When you develop them as part of your brand identity system, you can select among them every time you have a new communication that demands a texture.

You can apply them:

- to your social media backgrounds
- on PowerPoint or Keynote slides
- as a background for conveying quotes or stats.

Figure 8-1 shows what one of my quotes looks like on the background my company, Reach Personal Branding, uses.

Figure 8-1. Texture Use Example

Use textures that help you reinforce your brand message. For example, if you are all about technology, you could use a circuit board texture. If you're global, world maps might work.

Choosing Brand Images

You've heard the old adage "a picture is worth a thousand words." Images can go a long way to help you convey your message. So decide on the kinds of images that are right for your brand. First, decide if you prefer illustrations or photographic images. It's more of a personal choice—you just want a plan to use them consistently so it is easy for people to recognize materials that come from you.

Incorporate images as a part of every article or blog you create. According to contentmarketing.com, articles with images get 94 percent more total views. If you're going to go through all the work to write the article, add the picture to maximize the visibility.

So how do you find the images that are right for you? Here are some of my favorite free and royalty-free (or low-cost) resources for images:

- Pexels
- Unsplash
- Pixabay
- iStockPhoto.

In addition to the visual components, there are additional elements that will be important to you depending on what communications tools you plan to use to express your brand.

A Word About Packaging the Physical You

One of the questions I often hear as people are building their brand is: What should I wear? I don't want to look like I'm trying too hard, and I don't want to look like I don't care. Here's my advice. For starters, remember that this question is not just about the face-to-face world. Deciding what to wear while delivering that keynote address affects the digital you because you want to be photographed and filmed while that keynote is happening, don't you?

You might have your suits hemmed by a tailor, but "perfect fit" means much more than altering a seam. When you're trying to figure out your fashion factor, "tailor made" means choosing an outfit that sits at the intersection of these three criteria (Figure 8-2).

Figure 8-2. The Three Criteria of What to Wear

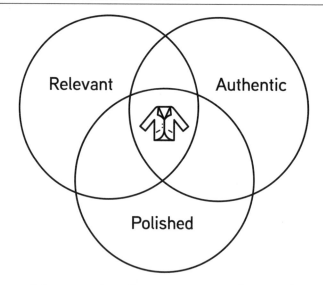

Relevant: It's appropriate for your target audience—those who are making decisions about you. If you're a sales exec selling to Silicon Valley startups, you might not need to wear a suit and tie or a skirt and heels, but if you're selling to banks in NYC, it might be the appropriate attire.

Authentic: It's on brand. In other words, it feels right. When you wear clothes that feel right, you're more confident, and you're likely reinforcing your brand. I worked with a coach who always wore a different, colorful, striking pin. It became the accessory everyone expected her to be wearing.

Polished: It's at the high end of the range of attire at your workplace. Every workplace has a range—on Wall Street, that range might be from sports coats and open-collar shirts to suit and tie or skirt with pumps. At a hip green manufacturing startup, the range might be shorts, T-shirt, and flip flops to khakis and a button-down shirt or slacks and a blouse. Put yourself on the higher end of the range.

REMOTE
CONTROL

Even when you're working from home, get dressed as if you're going into the office. First, it resets your mind. Second, when you are on videoconferences, you want to show up as professional (and you may be asked to join an unexpected video call at the last minute). One of the misconceptions about people working remotely is that they are less serious about work and are spending time doing things around the house while their on-site co-workers have their noses to the grindstone. Don't contribute to the stereotype of remote workers by showing up to videoconference calls in your jammies.

Apply Your PBID to Your Social Media Backgrounds

Whether someone is checking you out on LinkedIn or reading your tweets, you want them to have a similar visual experience. You do that by creating consistent backgrounds for the social media and other communications tools you plan to use. This includes LinkedIn, Twitter, YouTube, and Facebook.

Here are some tools that can help you create a compelling on-brand background for your social media profiles.

Canva: This design tool will allow you to create backgrounds easily. In the search box "What would you like to create," enter things like "LinkedIn banner," and it will produce a canvas with the proper dimensions.

PicMonkey: PicMonkey is an easy-to-use photo editor that allows you to access templates to create a custom background for your profiles thanks to creative tools for photo editing and graphic design. The collage maker feature allows you to upload and organize several images to create a truly customized background—one that can feature images that bolster your brand message.

Fotor: Fotor has a built-in option for creating backgrounds for your social media tools. This makes it easy to design something that you can use in all your online profiles, creating a consistent look across all your homes on the web. Choose the "cover photos" option and choose LinkedIn. Then drag the selected photos into the screen. The editing tools will help you refine your work of art.

Adobe Spark: Adobe Spark is a photo editing and design tool that also includes templates for some social media backgrounds. It has an inventory of images and allows you to upload your own.

PhotoFunia: This tool helps you make your mark with photos by incorporating them into mock-ups of spectacular background images including magazine covers, billboards, art galleries, and movie posters. PhotoFunia has a large variety of special effects that will attract attention. Combine the images you create here with the collage maker feature from PicMonkey to wow people who are checking you out.

PIXLR Express for Mobile: PIXLR is a mobile app that allows you to crop, create collages, and add effects to images you have.

You need not make your backgrounds identical. In fact, a little variation is helpful to make the banner relevant to the platform. But when you use your PBID to create them, it will be clear that all of your social media is connected to you.

All these tools are not only helpful with creating your background images (also called banners), they will also be valuable as you start to create visual posts for your social media accounts. We'll talk all about that in part 4.

Customize Your Email Signature

There's one more form of communications you must consider as a tool for conveying your brand, and that's the ubiquitous, somewhat dreaded email.

In addition to making sure what you say and how you say it reflect your brand, you have an opportunity to brand your emails with your e-signature. Your company could be anywhere on the scale when it comes to allowing you to customize your email signature, from "do whatever you want" to "follow this prescribed rule." For those of you who have some or total control, here are the ways you can customize your email signature (and remember, even if your company is really rigid about this, you should nonetheless brand your personal email signature).

The standard important stuff:

- **Your name** (the way you want people to use it) along with your job title and company.
- **Contact details.** Make it easy for people to connect with you. Include your business phone number, and include your company's website.
- **Logo.** Include your company logo.
- **Icons** with hyperlinks to your social media accounts, especially to your LinkedIn profile.

 REMOTE
CONTROL

Add your photo to your email signature. Remember, your colleagues don't get to see your smiling face at the coffee station at the office, so give them a subtle reminder of who you are by including your picture in your email signoff—if your company allows it.

Choosing Your Audio Elements

What's audio doing in a chapter about visuals? Audio is an important medium for bringing your brand to life because when people listen to your voice, they form a visual image of you in their mind's eye, and that enhances the emotional connection being formed throughout the development of your PBID.

How could you go about adding an audio element to your suite? One word: podcasts. They're a powerful vehicle for expressing your thought leadership. Twenty-seven percent of men and 24 percent of women listened to podcasts in the last month (Edison Research 2018). Monthly podcast listeners grew to 26 percent year over year (HubSpot 2018).

Writing Scripts

If you're a fan of podcasts and decide that it's a productive way for you to reach your target audience, then you're going to need great content. You may not have time to produce 30-minute podcasts on a regular basis (and your audience will only tune in for 30 minutes if the content is truly superb). A two- to five-minute message that delivers real insight on a regular basis is more likely to develop a following than an hour-long show of rambling and self-promotion.

Either way, you'll need a solid plan for each podcast. A script doesn't have to mean that you write down every word you want to say and then read the whole thing out loud. That might be effective if you have an engaging speaking voice, but a script can simply be your written plan for what your listeners will hear. You could start out with an ad lib before reading a series of eye-opening statistics on new developments in your field. You could use your podcast to call an expert, and (spreading the word about her brand, too, of course) you could record her answer to a question about a current topic in your industry. There are unlimited ingredients you could choose for your podcast. Just make sure you have a great game plan before you begin and choose ingredients that will resonate with your audience—while building a strong, memorable mental image of you.

Choosing Intro Tracks

Make sure to begin and end your podcast with an audio bumper (a special sound effect or series of musical notes that last for just a few seconds). This will create an aura of professionalism and polish, and this consistent audio cue will become associated with your personal brand. When used consistently, it will make your recording recognizable and memorable. Can you hum the four-note Intel inside sound?

My favorite site for royalty-free music is audiojungle.net. Search under logos and idents. Then choose the mood you're looking to convey.

Recording Audio

Your computer surely has a microphone, or you can activate a phone app to make your recording, but the principle of professional photographs holds true for recordings as well: Poor technical quality makes you look (and sound) like an amateur. A high-quality digital microphone, which you use to export the recording as an uploadable file, could be a good investment if you're not happy with the sound levels on your current devices.

And just as the background image for your headshot matters, the background noise for your audio matters, too—except that there shouldn't be any background noise. Always record in a space that's free of sirens, barking, and chattering.

Not sure how to blend your tracks (the bumpers, voice recordings, and other elements) into one podcast? Apple computers come with GarageBand, and PC users can download Audacity, a free open-source software. Both of these programs can be used for deleting a hiccup, fading the volume of your bumper music, and making other final edits. If this isn't how you want to spend your time, hire an audio editor who can mix your ingredients into a masterpiece worthy of your brand.

**BRANDI
BRAINSTORMS**

So what did Brandi include in her PBID?

- **Color:** Orange—because the word determination.
- **Fonts:** Avenir—a simple, modern font.
- **Textures:** Connoting both global and modern.
- **Images:** Brandi chose to go with photographic images instead of illustrations. Her reasoning—they are more sophisticated, and she can use her own personal library of photos she has taken from around the world.
- **Audio:** Brandi wants to eventually host a podcast with brief tips on how to collaborate and build harmonious teams.

Summing Up

Now you're convinced of how important packaging is to reinforcing your brand, and you've determined your brand color, fonts, and so forth. Bravo! Once you've applied your PBID to each of these elements—from the way you look to the way you sound—you've taken a major leap toward bolstering your brand with your community. And now you're ready to kick it up a notch. In chapter 9, you're going to put your brand in motion—motion pictures that is. We'll focus the entire chapter on the most powerful tool for delivering a complete and compelling message in the digital world: video. I'll convince you about the power of video and help you find the right video tools and formats to use to make your brand stand out, all in an accessible way so that even technology novices and technophobes can have fun working with this all-important medium.

CHAPTER 9

Use Rich Media to Engage and Connect

Get Ready For Your Close-Up

Video is vital. If you have read anything I have written over the past decade—in my Forbes column, my LinkedIn blog, or previous books—you know I am video's biggest fan. And that's because it is the single best opportunity for brand building, next to being there in person, of course. Look at the nine trends I shared at the start of this book, and you'll see that a majority of them are tied to the importance of video. In fact, one of the reasons remote work has become possible and more productive is because of the power and availability of all things video.

 **MINDSET RESET**

Video is not just for TV personalities, it's not reserved for CEOs, and it's not something to fear or avoid. Video is every career-minded professional's best friend and the most powerful tool for being real in the virtual world.

Eight Reasons to Choose Video

When I talk about video, I'm speaking about both synchronous video—using real-time, same-time communications tools like Webex, Skype, Join.me, Google Hangouts, Adobe Connect, and Zoom—and asynchronous video—producing, editing, and sharing videos on YouTube and via other social media. Both are important and valuable to your digital brand.

Synchronous video puts you in the conference room even when your home office is 2,000 miles away. It reminds people you're there and allows you to deliver more memorable messages when you're sharing updates on videoconference calls. Get in the habit of using video for your one-on-one calls and group meetings to increase your impact and help you stand out from your peers.

Asynchronous video is a powerful tool for demonstrating your thought leadership and making sure your communications stand out. It's more engaging than the written word and allows you to demonstrate your passion, energy, and personality in ways that are virtually impossible to do with articles, whitepapers, or other text-based forms of communication.

"Alright Mr. DeMille, I'm ready for my close-up."

Those were famous words uttered by Gloria Swanson at the end of the Billy Wilder movie (and more recently, the Broadway musical) *Sunset Boulevard.* But don't worry, you don't need to be a melodramatic, attention-driven actress like the character Norma Desmond. Quite the contrary, in fact. You'll be using video to connect with—and deliver value to—others.

 FUN FACT

1.8 million words: That's the value of one minute of video, according to Dr. James McQuivey in the Forrester research report, *How Video Will Take Over The World.*

Here's why you need to make video your BFF:

Video builds trust. Effective personal branding is all about connecting with others on a human level. Video is the next best thing to having a deeply connective human-to-human, face-to-face interaction. It allows you to engage with people on a much deeper level than text-based communications. It also conveys your personality in a way that text (and even audio alone) just can't. That's because video allows you to deliver a complete communication.

Video fosters teamwork. It's hard to feel part of a team when you're communicating exclusively by email, text, and instant messaging. But when you use video, you feel more connected and engaged with your co-workers. Polycom, a communications and technology company, learned from a global study that an astounding 92 percent of workers say that video collaboration actually improves their teamwork.

Video is differentiating. It helps you stand out from the myriad others who rely on the 26 letters of the alphabet to share their message. Many of your peers or competitors aren't using video yet. Most don't have a YouTube channel. That gives you an instant competitive edge when you incorporate video into your brand communications. This is critical because the world is getting more and more competitive. When you master video, you can distinguish yourself from everyone else who seemingly does what you do.

🛜 REMOTE
📱 CONTROL

Insist on having all your meetings via video. If you're in charge of the meeting, always choose a videoconference over a phone conference so you can "be there" even when you aren't. If you aren't running the meeting, suggest to the organizer that you use video.

Video is popular. Many people prefer video more than text as the medium for consuming information. A Cisco report states that "by 2020, there will be almost a million minutes of video per second crossing the Internet" (Doeing 2018). Video reaches 85 percent of the U.S. Internet population. According to *Forbes*, 59 percent of executives would rather watch video than read text. Every 60 seconds, 72 hours of video content is uploaded to YouTube, and 45 percent of people watch more than an hour of Facebook or YouTube videos a week (An 2018). Technically, YouTube is not a search engine, but according to Social Media Today, the number of daily searches on YouTube is greater than those on Yahoo and Bing combined (Hubspot 2018).

Video is essential. Video is being used to evaluate you. If you've been avoiding video, thinking that you can get by without ever looking into a camera, think again. Video is being used by companies in the hiring process. Companies like HireVue, Spark Hire, and videoBIO are working with organizations to completely transform the traditional interview. Some companies are using real-time video interviewing in lieu of flying you to their HQ. Others are relying on videos submitted by candidates with responses to a set of questions. How you perform in these videos will determine if you make it onto the shortlist—or not.

Video is easy. It's no longer hard to produce, edit, store, or share video. Not long ago, creating a quality video was a challenge. You needed to go into a studio, hire an editor, and expand your computer's storage. And sharing and watching video was frustrating because of bandwidth demands. Today, you can get similar results yourself thanks to built-in HD video cameras, video-editing apps, and social media platforms like YouTube. In addition, the formality of video is decreasing. More casual videos are not only acceptable, they are what we're becoming used to, thanks to our collective video-viewing habit of a billion hours of videos watched on YouTube daily (Heine 2017). Sure, a lot of those hours are spent watching hilarious dog tricks or Beyonce's latest music video. But YouTube is more than an entertainment platform. Every major corporation has a channel and so do most thought leaders.

Video is viral. When you go to the effort of creating brand communications, you want them to be received. Creating compelling video content that you share on your preferred social media channels will greatly outperform other forms of communications. That's because it allows you to engage others in expanding the visibility of your content. Social video generates 1,200 percent more shares than text and images combined (Mansfield 2019). On LinkedIn, video is shared 20 times more often than other content formats (Bunting 2018).

Video is the future. It's the fastest-growing form of communications. Video will represent 82 percent of all IP traffic in 2021 (*Business Insider* 2017). As companies continue to allow (or even encourage) their people to work remotely, their investment in video tools is increasing. Since it is likely that you will work remotely some or all of the time in the future, being skilled on these video platforms will be essential.

Still not sure if video is the right tool for you?

 PONDER THIS

Is video right for you? Track the number of times you answer "yes" to these questions:

- Am I—or could I become—comfortable in front of a camera?
- Am I a remote worker, spending more than half my time away from the office?
- Are the people I regularly work with (my team, clients, business partners) not co-located with me?
- Do I often have complex information, concepts, or stories to share?
- Would I like my communications to stand out from my peers' or competitors'?
- Do I often sell products, ideas, or plans?
- Would my audience prefer video to written communications?
- Am I more skilled at speaking or presenting rather than writing?
- Do I prefer speaking or presenting to writing?

- Am I looking to build my thought leadership or become known as a subject matter expert?

If you answered yes to any of these questions, consider video. If you answered yes to five or more of these questions—make video your medium!

Video is the next best thing to being there. So how can you use video to help you stand out and connect with people, specifically people who count?

12 Ways to Use Video on the Job

Here are some ways to incorporate video into your communications strategy that are clever, interesting, or easy to implement. Pick the ones that resonate with you and commit to making an impact with video.

1. Team update. Want your team to pay attention to your regular status messages? Use video. I have a client who has a global team. Only one member of her team is co-located with her. Each Sunday night, she creates a one-minute video from her living room letting her team know what happened in the past week, acknowledging great work from her people (calling them out by name), and letting them know what she's planning for the coming week. It has made her team feel more connected to her and to each other.

2. Community welcome. Recently, after accepting a LinkedIn connection request, I received a message from my new connection. It really stood out because it was a video "welcome to my community" message. He differentiated himself from my 30,000 LinkedIn connections because the video really let me get to know him and made me feel like I had met a real human being—not a robot.

3. Invitation. If you're holding an event or a special meeting, or you want to boost attendance at a webinar, a video invitation will feel more personal than one that is delivered as a regular boring email. When I was launching my last book, *Ditch. Dare. Do!*, I used a personal video message letting everyone know the fun things the launch party had in store. Over 80 percent of the people I invited attended. I'm pretty sure it was the power of video that got them there, but my co-author Deb Dib thought it was more likely the promise of cupcakes from my favorite NYC bakery, Billy's.

4. Thought leadership. The best way to show that you're an expert on a topic is to exude your enthusiasm and expertise through video. It's the ideal medium for demonstrating that you're an authority and expressing your point of view so you can attract followers and build your community within your area. One of my law firm clients uses video to introduce the whitepapers their lawyers create. The video highlights important points and introduces prospective clients to the author.

5. Video bio. Rather than (or in addition to) telling your story via a traditional text bio, tell the world who you are and what you're passionate about with a video bio. It will be easier for them to understand what you're about. And don't worry about sounding all "me, me, me." You can use phrases like, "I am so proud to be working with a team that . . ." and "I have had the privilege of working with some of the best . . ."

6. Vlog. Instead of having a blog, commit to video as your platform. If you prefer to speak rather than write, creating a vlog could be easier and more fun (in addition to being more fruitful). Vlogs need only be one to three minutes as long as they deliver value to your audience. And don't worry about having your own vlog site. YouTube is the perfect place to host and share your vlogs.

7. Pitches or proposals. When you're pitching an idea to your boss or seeking funding for your idea, or you want to get stakeholders to buy into your pet project, video will cut through the clutter. Video helps your ideas stand out and get noticed, evaluated, accepted, and, most important, funded (approved). So when you're facing competition and you want to win, get out the video camera.

FUN FACT

Viewers retain 95 percent of a message when they watch it in a video compared to 10 percent when reading it in text, according to *Forbes* (Stafford 2017).

8. Recommendations. To put yourself firmly behind someone, share a testimonial in video for impact. Recommendations help people validate what they say about themselves, and video recommendations—because they feature the actual recommender—have even more weight.

9. Live videos. LinkedIn Live is LinkedIn's version of Facebook Live, and it provides an opportunity to get in front of your connections and groups in a more interesting way. These live videos need not be polished or highly produced; they're best when they're pithy and timely. Posting a video while you're at an industry conference, for example, is a powerful and generous way to share that experience with others who are interested in the same topic but can't be there in person.

10. Meetings. Real-time video—using Skype, Google Hangouts, or the video features of web conferencing tools like Zoom, Webex, GoToMeeting, and Adobe Connect—is an efficient way to interact when you can't bring everyone together in person. These platforms allow participants to feel a stronger connection to the meeting. One of my clients who works in professional services is always traveling. To stay connected with her team, she uses FaceTime for her one-on-ones—often doing it from the lobby of a client or in a taxi on the way to the airport. She says it takes the mystery out of what she's doing when she's away. Her people experience her itinerant lifestyle vicariously. It also shows her people she always has time for them even when she's busy globetrotting. Video one-on-ones and conferences also prevent participants from multitasking. When participants know they can be seen, they're less likely to read their email or have extraneous conversations using instant messaging. That makes video meetings more productive than teleconferences.

🔒 BRAND HACK

Use a consistent backdrop. Make your video meeting space recognizable by always using the same background for each office. This helps remind people of you. For example, these days when I am not on the road, I split my time between New York City and Miami Beach. My backdrop for each city is a piece of art, but I use a different piece by a different artist for each city. Inevitably, I'll hear, "Oh, William, you're in Miami today" or "I see you're back in NYC." This little detail creates a sense of connection and familiarity.

11. Follow-up to meetings. Do you eagerly await the follow-up emails that come after many of the meetings you attend? Probably not! You can get more people to pay closer attention to your post-meeting content (including the action items that everyone committed to) via video. Using the word "video" in an email subject line boosts open rates and clickthrough rates. And if some things are better in written form—for example, legal content or complex data—consider a hybrid vmail-email message.

12. Acknowledgment. Email can be such an uninspiring form of communication that a thank-you message sent via email can seem almost insincere. When you want to send heartfelt thanks to a client, a member of your team, or your boss, consider video. It allows you to convey what you really feel, and you can include visual evidence of the impact the partnership, gift, or deed is making on your team. A video message says, "I took the time to show how much I really care." Recognizing your people for the work they do is part of every leader's job. How would you feel if you received a video message praising your accomplishments and expressing gratitude?

I'm so sanguine about how pervasive video will become in the future, I created a new company with my co-founder Ora Shtull—CareerBlast.TV—focused exclusively on video learning tools for career-minded professionals. I am so enthusiastic about video, I considered focusing this entire book on the topic of video for personal branding.

I'm so enthralled with video that I invested in lighting, tripods, and other equipment to build my own in-house video studio. I'm video's biggest fan!

You know who else is a big fan of video?

Google.

Seven Tips When Adding Videos to the Web

When you're building your personal brand, you want to make sure you're visible to the people who are making decisions about you. According to Forrester, videos are much more likely than text pages to get that coveted page-one slot in search results, thanks to universal search. Searchmetrics defines universal search as follows:

> In the context of search engine optimization, "Universal Search" (also called "Blended Search" or "Enhanced Search") refers to the integration of additional media like videos, images, or maps displayed above or among the organic (that is, unpaid) search results of search engines.

Instead of focusing on blogs, articles, and whitepapers, spend time creating a video bio or a series of thought-leadership videos or video interviews with thought leaders in your area of expertise. This is your best opportunity to stand out from the pack and increase your connections and influence. When it comes to building your brand on the web, showing up on page one of a Google search is important. Why? Because if you're not on page one, you're nearly invisible. In fact, the top three organic results capture 61 percent of all the clicks, according to a ProtoFuse study.

If you have a personal website, having video on the landing page of your site makes it sticky! According to Wistia, videos encourage 2.6 times more time spent on a home page (Ayres and Wellin 2017).

A great way to introduce yourself to visitors is with a video bio. In fact, you can create a video bumper (or ident) to add to your brand identity system. It's a quick five-to-10 second opening image or animation that precedes your content. Your bumper will use elements of you PBID—like color, font, and imagery—and become part of your overall brand packaging. If you're not familiar with the term video bumper, you certainly are with the bumpers themselves. Every time you watch a 21st Century Fox movie, for example, you see the search lights and hear *bum ba da bum*. You can use the same audio that you sourced in chapter 8 as part of your ident, adding pictures or video, creating even more consistency among your communications. iStockPhoto and others house royalty-free video footage that could be helpful.

Now that you're convinced, use these Google-friendly tips to increase the chances of getting your videos to appear on page one and beyond:

1. It's all in the name. When choosing filenames, use keywords that are relevant to the content and consistent with words people would use to find you in a Google search. For example, my video filenames contain the words "personal branding."

2. Brevity speaks louder. Keep your videos short. Videos up to two minutes long get the most engagement.

3. Quality trumps quantity. A small number of high-quality videos will build your brand, but a flood of mediocre videos may detract from it. Make your videos scream quality by focusing on the sound, lighting, and what's in the frame—and of course, the content. And remember to practice. When it comes to return on investment in a video, high technical quality will increase its popularity and ensure your brand is seen in the most positive light.

4. YouTube is the place to start. Create a YouTube channel and host your videos there. Remember, YouTube is owned by Google, and YouTube videos often show up on page one. In other words, no matter what a person is searching for online, it's highly likely that they will come across some sort of video content early in their results, and 80 percent of these video results come from YouTube.

5. Keywords are . . . key. Make sure your video description is detailed, and choose tags related to how you want to be known, along with the words people would use to find you. When you are sharing your video using various social media, remember to use all the right hashtags.

6. Repurposing amps up visibility. Embed your YouTube videos in your website or blog and in the summary or experience section of your LinkedIn profile. LinkedIn allows you to integrate images and video directly into your profile. And, because most people aren't using this feature, it helps your profile stand out.

7. The 80/20 rule applies. When you do the work to create the video, spend extra time maximizing its visibility with your stakeholders. Promote the video to your network and stakeholders so it gets the most views possible. Spend 20 percent of your time in the creation of your video and 80 percent getting the right people to see it.

BRAND HACK

Create your own mini video studio that's ready to go 24/7. Make it easy to shoot video when the mood strikes and you have something you want to say to your brand community. Get on a last-minute video call with confidence by creating a space where you know the lighting is going to be great, the audio will be clear and free from background noise, and what's hanging on the wall behind you won't detract from your message. Then you have the perfect spot where you can shine at any time. When you make it easy to shoot video, you'll be more likely to use it.

Seven Final Thoughts for Leading the Video Vanguard

One of the most effective ways to build your brand is to demonstrate how innovative you are by planning and implementing a team-, division-, or company-wide initiative. Make video a part of your initiative—or make it the initiative.

These seven tips will help ensure that your videos build your brand with those who are making decisions about you:

1. Start with a bang. You have less than 10 seconds to grab viewers' attention.

2. Know your message and take a stand. Your video can be an opportunity to demonstrate your thought leadership, express your unique point of view, and communicate what you believe and how you deliver value.

3. Keep it short and sweet. Keep your video to a maximum of two to three minutes. Attention spans are short and shrinking. Say what you want to say, and don't waste a second. It's OK—in fact, it's valuable—to leave them wanting more.

4. Dress for the occasion. Reflect your personal brand while being relevant to the audience you want watching your video. Don't wear clothes with stripes, prints, or busy patterns. Remember to use makeup to ensure you're not shiny. Catharine Fennell, CEO of VideoBio, recommends Makeup Forever Professional HD Translucent Powder. These small details will all contribute to a polished product.

5. Choose what surrounds you. What you have behind you speaks about your brand. Make sure your setting reinforces your brand message and doesn't distract the viewer. You want people to focus on you and what you're saying, not the books that are teetering on the shelf behind you. Consider using your brand color to create recognition and memorability.

6. Hire the professionals. Make an investment in yourself and your career by investing in one high-quality video bio made by a professional production company, which is also worthwhile for any other really important, high-impact video you might decide to create. Use a comprehensive service or bring together the right experts, including a coach to help you with your script, a camera person, a professional video editor, and so on.

7. Maximize distribution. Now that you've spent time and effort producing your primary video (most likely a bio), amp up the dividends by making sure it gets seen by those who need to know you. Post your masterpiece to multiple video sites, including your own website and YouTube. Make your video part of your LinkedIn profile and your blog. Include it in your email signature and put the link at the top of your resume. Be sure that the sites where you post your video are targeting a relevant audience.

Still reluctant to get in front of the camera?

Although being on camera is ideal because that's what creates the emotional connection between you and the viewer, if you are convinced you aren't telegenic (it's probably not true!) or you just abhor the idea of being filmed, produce compelling videos using still images (photos or other graphics) and stock video. Create a PowerPoint or Keynote presentation with voice-over to get your message across. Even if you don't appear on camera, this format provides a much richer medium for conveying your message than text alone.

And if recording a voice-over doesn't feel right, don't worry. Using subtitles can still get your message across. In fact, this silent-movie approach reflects the trends of how many people prefer to experience their videos. Eighty percent of videos on LinkedIn are watched with sound off, and 85 percent of videos on Facebook are watched without sound (Patel 2016). This form of video content (images or stock video footage with subtitles) is becoming so popular, there are companies springing up—like Animoto, Videolicious, and Lumen5—with templates and tools to make the development process simple.

**BRANDI
BRAINSTORMS**

Brandi decided that video is a powerful way for her to amp up her brand trait of "persuader." She decided to incorporate these video elements into her brand communications strategy:

- All my client pitches will include a video story.
- My monthly team meetings will now be done in a conference room with a video wall and my remote team members will appear "on the big screen."
- I'll post to my LinkedIn feed live videos from my global travels— sharing relevant, valuable learning while highlighting the fact that I'm a citizen of the world!

Summing Up

Ready for your close up now?

I hope you're convinced that video is the most powerful digital branding vehicle and you're enthusiastic about executing your own video strategy. The more you integrate it into your communications, the easier it will become and the more polished you'll appear. With that behind you, we're going to move to the final frontier. Part 4 is where you'll learn everything you need to know to truly showcase your message. You'll go from being merely a distinguished brand to becoming a brand in demand. We'll start by building your fan club in chapter 10.

Part 4
Social You

The key to successful leadership today is influence, not authority.
—Ken Blanchard

PART 4

Social You

This final section focuses on leadership—social leadership, to be exact. Whether you have an official leadership role in your organization or not, you can (and should) be a leader. Specifically, we'll discuss leading with expertise. This means building and nurturing your network by sharing your thought leadership. It also means demonstrating that you are a socially savvy leader by becoming a digital brand ambassador for your organization.

CHAPTER 10

Assess Your Current On- and Offline Networks

Build Your Fan Club

Now that you have some clarity about your message thanks to your exploration in part 1, and you've presented your message digitally and visually (parts 2 and 3), let's talk about growing the audience for that message. And with that comes growth in branding—the taller the tree, the longer the shadow. When you grow and foster strong, enduring relationships, you move yourself across the branding continuum toward the ultimate goal in branding—being a brand in demand (Figure 10-1).

Figure 10-1. The Branding Continuum

You	Sales: Transactional	Marketing: Relational	Branding: Attractive
	01 Undifferentiated	**02** Distinguished	**03** Demanded
Offering	Commodity: Meets the Need	Customized: Delivers Extra Value	Branded: Creates a Unique Experience
Decision Makers	Clients	Fans	*Promoters*

With your brand promise crystal clear in the hearts and minds of the people who need to know you, you can create a magnetic field that attracts opportunities. In chapter 2, you defined your brand community, or 5 D team (decision makers, doyens, disciples, defenders, and discoursers). In this chapter, I'm going to help you build and nurture that Dream Team so you can expand your visibility and your level of connection.

As we discussed in chapter 2, selective fame is all about being visible and available to your target audience—the people who will influence your success. The web provides infinite opportunities for you to expand that team. Before we get to growing your network, it's time to add one more D to your Dream Team. That final D is for diversity. Although personal branding means focusing on your target audience, there's equal value in diversifying your network.

According to Ivan Misner—called the "Networking Guru" by *Entrepreneur* magazine—"A diverse personal network enables you to increase the possibility of including connectors, or linchpins, in your network. Linchpins are people who in some way cross over between two or more clusters or groups of individuals. In effect, they have overlapping interests or contacts that allow them to link groups of people together easily" (Misner 2004). And former Merrill Lynch global wealth head Sallie Krawcheck shared on LinkedIn: "If my network is made up solely of female financial services professionals of my generation, who all hail from the South, I will likely feel very comfortable with them. And I will likely enjoy my time with them. And I will no doubt learn from them. But at some point, this will become an echo chamber of similar-enough experiences and perspectives."

In fact, a study published in the *Journal of Corporate Finance* and quoted in *Harvard Business Review* underscored this concept, finding that "CEOs with strong connections to people of different demographic backgrounds and skill sets create higher firm value."

MINDSET
RESET

In building your network, you need to be both focused on your target and open to meeting new people who are different from you. In fact, when it comes to building your network on LinkedIn, my mantra is "be promiscuous."

✔ **DO THIS,**
✘ **NOT THAT**

Do establish your criteria and accept LinkedIn connections from all the people who meet those criteria, regardless of whether you know them well or not. Criteria can include things like: We work in the same industry. Or we have five people in common. Or they seem legitimate—they are very engaged.	**Don't** shut out unexpected opportunities by being too restrictive in how you build your network; don't keep it "pure."

As a bonus, "being promiscuous" will help you build diversity into your network, and it's particularly helpful when it comes to LinkedIn. Here's why. When LinkedIn shows the results of a keyword search, the results are partially based on the level of connection between the person doing the search and the people who turn up in the results. So, the more connections you have, the more times you'll show up in search results, and the higher you'll rank in those results—ultimately delivering the most opportunities for people to be able to connect with you.

Creating an Open Network

Numerous studies show that the number 1 predictor of success is simply being in an open network instead of a closed one (Simmons 2015).

BRAND
HACK

Connect with the connected. When you connect with people who have a lot of connections or followers, you become visible to a much larger, more diverse community. Their network members become more aware of what you're doing (in LinkedIn, this happens because they become your second-level connections), and that helps you grow your network's depth and breadth, allowing greater potential diversity in your network.

Here's how to build your focused-yet-open network with all the right Ds. This exercise is divided into three parts: past, present, and future.

Start With Your Past

Get your online network in parity with the real-world connections you've developed throughout your career. For all your social media accounts that you plan to use, search and find the people you:

- have worked with in the past
- went to school with
- met through volunteering and similar activities.

In other words, take a trip down memory lane.

In LinkedIn, you can import your email addresses and iPhone contacts to make this process easier. This will allow you to reach out to a large number of contacts at once, no matter how long you have known them.

Once you're up-to-date, focus on the present.

BRAND HACK

Face the future by looking at the past. Reverse sort your email so the oldest messages show up on top. Then, look through the names of the senders who contacted you a while ago. Make it a goal to reconnect with the ones you've lost touch with. Add them to your digital-brand community.

Broaden With the Present

Build your network deliberately. To get the right people in your network—the decision makers and influencers who can help you reach your goals—

begin by performing a gap analysis. Go back to the 5Ds and document your peeps in the five areas. When you know who is in your network, you can identify missing links. You might identify these missing connections by name, job title, industry, and so forth. Then proactively build your network. In all your chosen social media platforms, use hashtags to find people by shared interest, and then add, follow, or connect as appropriate.

Play With the LIONs

LIONs are LinkedIn Open Networkers. This is not a designation that was bestowed on them by LinkedIn. Members decide for themselves whether they want to be a LION or not. LIONs—as their name implies—are delighted to accept connection requests from virtually any other member. To find LIONs, perform a search on people, select the "All filters" option and enter "LION" in the last name field.

I can hear what you are thinking right now: "But I don't want just anyone in my network; I only want relevant people." Not to worry. To get to just those LIONs who are relevant to you and your career or business, use additional filters—you can choose locations, industries, and so forth. Then your search will yield a list of open networkers who would be valuable to add to your network. Send connection requests to add them to your growing list.

 BRAND HACK

Easily add LinkedIn connections. When you reach out directly to a new contact, don't send a connection request by clicking "connect" from their profile. Instead, send your connection requests through search. If you connect through a person's profile, LinkedIn requires that you show how you are connected (via a company you worked for or a school you attended). That's not required when you use search. Search for the person you want to connect with, and then click "connect" next to their name in the search results. Remember to customize all LinkedIn requests; avoid the generic invitation.

Plan for the Future

With your online network current and a plan in place to create growth, put systems in place to keep it that way.

Make Meetings Matter

Every time you meet someone you would like to have in your network, reach out immediately. Or better yet, keep the LinkedIn app open on your phone and add them as soon as you meet them. Turn this into a ritual so you will always keep your network up-to-date.

 BRAND HACK

Use the LinkedIn QR code to connect in real time (and to show how digital savvy you are!). The QR code is the best way to add people to your network immediately upon meeting them. And as an extra bonus, using this feature demonstrates that you're socially savvy—putting yourself in the category of "innovative" in the mind of your new contact.

In the LinkedIn app on your phone, you'll find your unique code at the top on the right side of the search bar. Tap on it, choose "my code," and the image will be displayed at a size that will make it easy for people to scan it. Here's mine:

William Arruda
Personal branding pioneer, motivational
speaker & author: helping professional...

Put Others to Work

You can accelerate the growth of your network by enlisting others in your mission. They'll be happy to help when you make it easy for them. Here's how.

Add a direct link in your email signature to your preferred social media accounts. Including a link to your LinkedIn profile will help people get to know you.

Ask people to connect with you when you deliver presentations or web conferences. Include a slide at the end requesting that the audience members connect with or follow you.

Put your social media contact details on your real-world communications materials like your business cards, letterhead, thank you cards, and more.

BRAND HACK

Keep your contacts in one place. Maintain your own professional contact management system in LinkedIn. You can add your contacts to your connections and LinkedIn followers by connecting your LinkedIn account with your email and phone contacts. Then, you have all your people in one place. People change jobs, and their emails change as well—making it hard to stay in touch. That's less likely to happen with their LinkedIn profile, as long as they keep it updated.

Just remember to export a backup copy of your LinkedIn community every six months or so. This way, you always have a list of your contacts just in case LinkedIn is unavailable. Downloading backup copies is a good habit to form for all your important cloud-based information.

Maximizing LinkedIn Groups

In LinkedIn, the easiest way to find "your people" is by joining groups. When you engage in groups, you can start to identify the people you'd like to stay in touch with. Groups are like professional associations online, with three big benefits:

- They usually have a lot more members. Some groups have hundreds of thousands of members who are all interested in a specific topic.
- They're 24/7. Unlike real-world associations with monthly meetings, you can engage and connect when it's convenient for you.
- Although they are focused on one topic, their members are often more diverse than in traditional professional associations, including a variety of people from various parts of the world, who all share an interest in the topic.

LinkedIn allows you to belong to 100 groups. Join groups related to different aspects of your life. These may include:

- alumni (schools and previous companies)
- thought leadership (your area of expertise, industry, and job function)
- social causes (philanthropy, volunteer groups, and so forth)
- interests and passions
- local groups (New York City Running Club, for example).

You want the right mix of groups to help showcase your personal brand. The groups you belong to not only allow you to increase your visibility and build relationships with others, but they also say something about who you are and what's important to you. When someone looks at the groups you've joined, they make a determination about who you are based on the company you keep. Here's the process:

1. Research. For each of the categories, research potential groups. Type the appropriate keywords in the search box at the top of the LinkedIn page, search, and then click on "more" and click "groups." You'll get a list of relevant groups along with the number of members. Briefly explore your options by reading the descriptions of the groups.

2. Join and lurk. Join the groups that meet these criteria:

- They have a high number of members who meet your criteria.
- The members are active, adding content and comments regularly. Belonging to inactive groups is like attending a networking function where no one shows up or people aren't really engaged.
- The content resonates with you. You're learning from true thought leaders and have an interest in sharing your own opinions and ideas.

Spend time understanding the culture of the group, discovering which members are most active, and finding out which topics generate the most engaging content. You can hang out in the background for a bit to acclimate yourself.

3. Introduce yourself. Just as you'd do at a professional association meeting, let people know who you are and that you are thrilled to become part of the conversation. Introduce yourself to the group and let them know why you are excited to be a part of their community. Other group members will likely reach out to you—and that will be a great opportunity to grow your relationships within the group.

4. Become an active member. Only after you have completed the previous steps can you start to maximize the value of groups. In the next chapter, I share ways to tap the full potential of groups.

5. Join the conversation. Before posting any of your own content, comment on others' and use the "like" button. It's much like the art of real networking. You shouldn't rush into a group that is already formed and start speaking. Listen first.

6. Be consistent. When you join a group (online or not), become a regular part of the community. Set up a weekly calendar reminder. Consistency builds brands. You will see little benefit in being an intermittent member who posts and reads without regularity.

7. Identify brand community members. You will start to identify people who can fit into your 5 D brand community strategy: mentors, business partners, future hires, colleagues, trusted advisors, and mentees. Add these people to your LinkedIn connections, and reach out to them occasionally to build and maintain these relationships.

Learn About Others

Another great aspect of networking is getting to know others. You can check out people who are on a meeting attendee list that you haven't met or learn about prospective clients, research competitors, and identify and source the ideal candidates for open roles. Use it before meetings to get the 4-1-1 on the people you're about to meet. Find common connections and interests and start building stronger relationships.

BRAND HACK

Research on the DL. For those times where you want your sleuthing to be on the down-low (especially if you're looking to poach talent or check out a competitor), be sure to change your privacy setting in the profile viewing options to "private mode."

Summing Up

Can you hear your fans applauding your accomplishments? All strong brands have a fan club of people who know who they are and respect them for their expertise and point of view. When you build your network and stay connected to your network members, you make them aware of your expertise and your viewpoints on pertinent topics. This external community of people becomes a valuable asset as you progress in your career. But building and nurturing your fan club is just one step in the process of becoming a demanded brand. The next (and crucial!) step involves turning those fans into promoters so you have a full-time sales force touting your brilliance.

CHAPTER 11

Nourish and Mobilize Your Network

Turn Fans Into Promoters

Don't toot. Let others tout.

Now that you have updated your network and are actively building it, you need to nurture those relationships, increasing your visibility and credibility to get the people who know and like you to promote you. In a sense, you're creating your own personal sales force of professionals who are eager to tout your brilliance so you don't have to toot your own horn. This is always a welcomed message by my friends who consider themselves introverts. No chest pounding. No screaming from rooftops. No "me-me-me" required. The technique you'll use to groom promoters also happens to be my favorite four-letter word:

Give.

And when you give in this case, you're giving value—helping others be more successful, and further reinforcing that message you crafted in chapter 3 by sharing your intellectual property.

In the field of branding, this is called content marketing. The definition of *content marketing* (from dictionary.com) is "a type of marketing that involves the creation and sharing of online material (such as videos, blogs, and social media posts) that does not explicitly promote a brand but is intended to stimulate interest in its services." In this case, the "service" is you.

MINDSET RESET

Whether your role is in legal, accounting, or product development, you're a marketer. You're the CMO of the brand called *You!*

The goal of content marketing is to get your audience to engage with your material. It makes no sense to spend time and money on creation and curation if it doesn't affect the people you seek to influence. Creating this engagement is challenging because there's so much noise. We are bombarded with an ever-increasing amount of content to absorb.

FUN FACT

500 million tweets are sent, over 95 million photos and videos are shared on Instagram, and over 4 million blog posts are published every day.

And the noise is getting louder. The only thing no one is making more of is time. My biggest fantasy is to be able to buy time. I think about it a lot—perhaps too much! I'd buy an hour most mornings for some extra sleep and I would have bought hundreds of hours while writing this book. My clients tell me they would likely buy an hour a day or so to spend building their brand. But until that dream becomes a reality, we still have just 24 hours a day. That means as a content creator, you're facing increasing competition for eyeballs with no increase in the amount of time you have to build your brand.

Update, Create, Curate, Restate, Evaluate

When building a brand communications plan that connects with your people, focus on a series of actions I call the Five Ate Plates. Think of it as a carefully crafted five-course tasting menu in a world overrun by generic junk food. All five actions end in "ate," and they are all designed to serve up nutrient-rich messages that your audience is actually craving.

You'll find a lot of analogies and references in this chapter to food—which will hopefully whet your appetite to try some of the activities that will help you build a sales force of people who can help you spread your message.

The ideal communications plan uses a balanced combination of these techniques to build engagement with your target audience. Let's look at each one individually.

Plate 1: Update

The purpose of updating is to remain visible to your community. The third of the 3 Cs of a strong brand is constancy—staying in the purview of your target audience (Figure 11-1).

Figure 11-1. The 3 Cs of Personal Branding

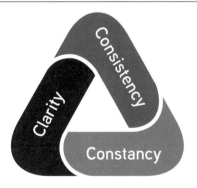

Updates can come in the form of LinkedIn posts, tweets, Facebook, and LinkedIn live videos, and so forth. But use them in moderation. Don't update because you've told yourself you have a quota to meet. Instead, provide information that's relevant and timely—content that helps keep your audience up to date.

Effective updates can include:
- pointing to a newly published article
- checking in at a relevant location—like a professional association event
- sharing something you learn from a workshop
- linking to a quick live video with a valuable insight from a conference you're attending.

When you share an update, you're making your connections and followers aware of what's going on in your world, providing knowledge that could be valuable to them. Sharing an update is the best way to let them know what's going on in your world. It's the digital equivalent of a postcard. Just sharing a few sentences—"I learned at yesterday's AMA meeting that marketers are going to spend 20 percent more on video in 2020"—is a simple yet powerful way to deliver value to decision makers while staying on their radar.

Plate 2: Create

Content creation takes a lot more time than updating, but it is one of the most powerful ways to differentiate your expertise and get people to know you and want to support you. The LinkedIn long-form publishing platform gives you the opportunity to convey your thought leadership and remain visible. It also helps you enhance your credibility by backing up what you say in your profile with your content and your unique point of view. And you can make your thoughts known to half a billion members—growing your reach. Of course, you don't need all of them to look at your content. You just want to attract the members of your 5D community (remember selective fame?). So here's some good news: While the content noise is increasing, only 1 million LinkedIn members have ever published a blog on the platform, according to the content marketer Foundation. That's less than 0.2 percent of LinkedIn members. That means there's still an opportunity to be a leader on the platform.

It's very easy to use (you can paste content from a Word file)—and your posts only need to be between 600 and 1,000 words. When you use this feature regularly, it becomes a repository of your ideas on your preferred topic. Just remember, don't blow hot air. What you share needs to be a clear reinforcement of your brand message (how you want to be known), while ultimately delivering valuable information to your target audience. Emphasize potency, not puffery.

Content creation can include:

- writing a blog post for LinkedIn
- producing a thought-leadership video for YouTube
- publishing the PDF of a slide presentation to SlideShare
- creating an infographic and posting it on Instagram.

REMOTE CONTROL

To give your content more impact, use richer forms of communication—especially video—so the people you work with get to know you better. Combine words, images, and videos to deliver a compelling message.

Because content creation takes more time and effort, you want to make sure it's going to yield high levels of engagement and support your goal of inspiring people to become your brand ambassadors. To help you reap a higher return on your investment of energy, I created the Strawberry Test. It's a way to find the "sweet spot" in your messaging.

Although you need to be aware of the kinds of content you like to create and what your target audience desires, certain types of content have been shown to attract the most engagement (measured by views, likes, comments, and shares). High-engagement content sits at the intersection of three traits (Figure 11-2): inviting, bite-sized, and healthful.

Figure 11-2. The Strawberry Test

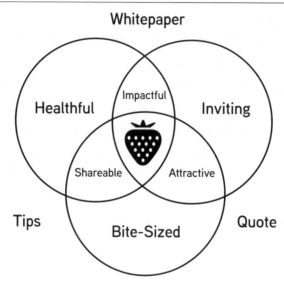

Inviting. With so much content vying for our attention, we are only attracted to the truly enticing messages. In a split second, we'll decide whether to keep reading—or not—so the message needs to be immediately compelling. This means your headline, caption, or intro words have the most crucial part of your content. (More about that in a moment, when you'll learn how to add your own secret sauce.)

Bite-sized. In our world of 280-character tweets, two-minute YouTube videos, and Snapchat pics that last for just seconds, we want content that doesn't require a major time commitment. It needs to satisfy—but quickly. If it's a full-blown whitepaper, the executive summary or bulleted list of takeaways needs to be succinct.

Healthful. "What's in it for me?" is the mindset and mantra of most social media viewers. People will only invest in your content if they believe they'll get something from it. They may want to learn and grow, solve a problem, or relieve stress with laughter. This is the "nourishment" element. That's why you need to ask yourself the following question:

How can my content help the reader or viewer?

Your answer determines whether it's worth your effort to produce that content. The level of viral sharing gained by a message is directly proportional to how valuable the message is to your target community. And the payoff needs to be obvious at the beginning of your content (think goldfish!). People aren't likely to stick with you until the end if they don't get connected at the beginning.

I've often thought that the most potentially viral content is like a strawberry. Strawberries are inviting, bite-sized, and healthful.

Of course, when you're creating content, not everything can be a strawberry—and it doesn't have to be. But seek to develop materials that meet at least two of the three characteristics.

Twizzlers: Inviting and Bite-Sized

Twizzlers (my favorite candy!) meets two of the criteria. But they're full of empty calories. Where's the health (value)? Think of this as a quote that you've added to an interesting background (using your PBID texture). It's visual and interesting—but it doesn't provide the viewer with anything earthshakingly valuable.

Watermelon: Inviting and Healthful

Some content, like a whitepaper, is more like a watermelon. It's sweet (inviting), but not exactly quick to consume, requiring a real commitment. Sometimes, though, this is what's required to get your message across.

Prunes: Bite-Sized and Healthful

There's some valuable content you'll want to create that does not require a major commitment to consume. But it may not be the most instantly enticing material. For example, a list of helpful tips.

Chocolate-Dipped Strawberry: Inviting, Bite-Sized, and Healthful

To make your content even more attractive and hopefully viral, dip it in chocolate. Think of the chocolate coating as the headline or title and first few sentences (or seconds of a video) and the associated image—drawing in the viewer the same way the chocolate-covered strawberry in the Godiva store window calls you in from the street.

 FUN FACT

Advertising pioneer David Ogilvy said, "On the average, five times as many people read the headline as read the body copy. When you've written your headline, you have spent 80 cents out of your dollar."

The "inviting" element is most important because without it, people are less likely to make that initial interaction, no matter how valuable and easy to consume your content is. So when creating content, put your fresh-picked words (or images) through my Strawberry Test. And don't publish them without dipping them in a rich chocolate coating.

Plate 3: Curate

If you're feeling like you don't have the time or desire to create your own content, steal other people's content. OK, I don't really mean "steal"; it's more like borrowing. Content curation can be your best friend when you are loath to create your own material. Share others' posts, disseminating information that you find interesting and valuable with your connections and groups. When you do, you're enabling them to see potentially helpful content that they otherwise might have missed. Most websites that distribute content, like *Forbes, Inc.,* and *Fast Company,* make it easy for you to share their content via LinkedIn, Twitter, and Facebook directly from what you're viewing.

✔ **DO THIS,**
✘ **NOT THAT**

Do offer your point of view with your commentary; for example: "This is a really useful article, especially for first-time managers."	**Don't** just click "share" without adding your unique perspective.

A word of caution: If you just click "share" and send content to your connections and groups, it does little to build your brand. You need to add your commentary and point of view—why you think it is valuable. For example, you might say, "This is a really useful article, especially the last paragraph." Or "This piece is a powerful overview; the only thing I would add is . . ." Or "This is a well-written piece, but I disagree with the author about her second point because . . ."

Plate 4: Restate

My personal branding technique for expanding visibility with minimal effort is called—wait for it—being lazy. By that I mean reusing and repurposing the content you already have available. This amplifies your message and delivers brand consistency, communicating different forms of the same content in distinctive ways to the members of your brand community. So repurpose your blog posts for your activity updates, turn an article into a series of tweets, and embed whitepapers and articles in the Summary and Experience sections of your LinkedIn profile. Never look at any piece of content you create in isolation. Always ask yourself, "How can I reuse this content to increase my visibility and add value to my brand community?"

Plate 5: Evaluate

It's powerful and even fun to regularly share your knowledge—and have conversations—with your community, but to what end? Get ready for the final course in our tasting menu: metrics.

You need to measure the effectiveness of your activities and the power of your digital brand. This allows you to focus on those activities that have proven to deliver the greatest impact on your career success, and it lets you ditch those that just aren't working for you.

The great news about digital branding is that most of what you can do can be measured, so you can check in on how your personal brand is growing.

Here are the metrics to check regularly:

- network growth
- LinkedIn visibility
- engagement
- opportunity.

Network Growth

Social media people metrics are calculations related to the number and types of people in your brand community. That includes both connections and followers.

If you're active in your field and the related online communities, your network should be growing. In LinkedIn, you can have up to 30,000 connections. So remember to add people to your LinkedIn network as you meet them. And reach out to those LinkedIn members you'd like to have in your network. Track your number of connections over time to ensure it's growing. Do the same with your Twitter followers, YouTube subscribers, SlideShare followers, and so forth.

If you're adding content to your social media accounts regularly, and you're engaging in discussions with fellow members, you should see your numbers increasing.

LinkedIn Visibility

Who's viewed your profile? This is an important number to watch over time. The more engaged you are in LinkedIn, the more this number should increase. If you haven't paid close attention to this number, find it (it's the first number you see when you look in the left column on the home page). Then make a commitment to check it out weekly or monthly to see if your LinkedIn actions are translating into more people checking you out.

Search appearances is a measure that also helps you see if people are able to find you. It increases when the words in your profile (especially in your headline) match the words people are typing into the search box. Targeted networking is important. It's also important to help people find you. I call it planned serendipity. You don't know who's looking for you, but you need to be visible and available so they can find and connect with you. Know the keywords that are critical for being found in your field and make sure your profile is replete with them—especially your headline. Also, remember that the more connections you have, the higher you will rank in searches, and the number of connections you have also affects how frequently you turn up in searches.

"People also viewed" is an important section to check regularly. It's located in the left column of the home page. Take a look, then ask yourself these questions: Are these people in my community? Are there other thought leaders and experts with whom I'd like to be associated?

Engagement

This is the all-important measure because it focuses on interaction and endorsement. The industry term for this is social proof, and achieving "proof" sometimes depends heavily on perception. According to Robert Cialdini, professor emeritus of psychology and marketing at Arizona State University and the author of *Influence: The Psychology of Persuasion,* "We view a behavior as more correct in a given situation to the degree that we see others performing it." That means in situations where we feel hesitant or insecure, we often assume that those in our orb (thought leaders, colleagues, superstars, and so forth) are more knowledgeable about the topics related to that situation.

That said, for digital branding, my ultimate goal is community minded. Thought leadership shouldn't be about exploiting the insecurity of your followers; it should be about empowering all members of the community to share their knowledge and gain influence through their bona fide expertise. So I abide by a narrower definition:

Social proof is external validation of your positive influence on the people in your brand community, demonstrating that you led them to support and engage with your brand while enhancing their own brand.

Here are four types of social proof that are relevant to career-minded professionals who are building their digital brand:

Expert Endorsement. This is when respected members of your industry or topic recommend you and your content. We talked about this kind of social proof in chapter 6 when we referenced raving recommendations—getting testimonials from people who count and posting them to your LinkedIn profile. It's called brand association. When you are connected to an organization, title, and company that's respected, some of that rubs off on you. You see this form of brand association all the time but may not realize it. When you stay at a Shangri-La hotel, there are Bulgari toiletries in the bathroom. The placement of those products reinforces the brand attribute of luxury with the Shangri-La.

Community Connection. This proof comes from the numbers. When you have a lot of Twitter followers or LinkedIn connections, people assume "you're somebody" and will be more likely to follow you and your content. In

LinkedIn, the Endorsements feature plays a role here. Your overall number of endorsements isn't very important. The number of endorsements for your most important skills, on the other hand, is extremely important—especially for your top three, because they're the only ones people see when they check out your profile (unless they click "see more"). Nothing attracts a crowd like a crowd, but in personal branding we need to focus on attracting the right crowd of decision makers who are just as committed to your field as you are.

Social Interaction. This comes in the form of views, likes, and comments on your content. When you have posted a YouTube video and it gets 1,000 views, that number alone is an endorsement of the video.

Social Volley. This is a special kind of social interaction because it creates the much-desired viral element of social media. It's all about shares. This social action is different from "social interaction" described above because it more rapidly moves you from the second to the third phase of brand success—where others become your personal brand sales team.

Shares are important because they speak to how viral your content is. When people share your content, they're making it available to their connections—significantly amping up its visibility. That's when your fans become promoters and actively share your content with their brand community.

Opportunity

This is a more qualitative measure. Since you started putting effort into building a socially engaged brand, what opportunities have come your way? To determine these, think about your goals. Why are you building your brand? What kinds of opportunities are valuable to you? You might consider these measures:

- requests to speak at events
- press outreach for quotes or interviews
- authors seeking content for an upcoming book (or a co-author)

- job offers or messages from recruiters
- messages from fans who want to work on your team
- colleagues with expertise who want to partner on a project
- internal colleagues reaching out because of your external visibility.

PONDER THIS

Ask yourself, what's building my social proof?
- What topics generate the most engagement?
- Which type of content (long articles, brief how-tos, lists, very technical explanations) has the biggest impact?
- Which medium is most engaging (blogs, videos, infographics, tweets)?
- What content is getting the most interaction: content I create or the content I curate?
- What content has received the highest number of shares?

Tips for Mastering Your Content Marketing

For maximum effectiveness, each of the first four "ate" actions—update, create, curate, restate—should be infused with the following four qualities:

Be authentic. Before you start posting, think about how you will exude your personal brand in your communications. You want to be memorable, so know your writing style and use it consistently. If humor is part of your brand, write with wit. If structure and organization are your thing, organize your content with headings and lists. If you are more of the contrarian, make that a regular part of your commentary. And throughout the message itself, of course, choose a voice that's authentic. If you really can't tell a joke, don't try to be Ellen DeGeneres—only Ellen can be Ellen.

Be professional. When posting your own content, make sure it is grammatically correct and written in the style used by your industry. Posting questions to the group is a great way to spur conversation around a specific topic and see your colleagues' various points of view, but even a one-sentence message like that should be proofread carefully.

Be engaged. When someone takes the time to comment on your post, take the time to respond. It's the right thing to do, and it helps you build relationships with those who are interested in your content while keeping the conversation going.

Be appreciative. Remember to acknowledge and thank those who post valuable comments and who add to the conversation in your posts. It's especially important to thank those who share your content. Also, thank your fellow group members who provide content you find useful in doing your job or expanding your mind.

Summing Up

Now you've identified your strategy for being ever visible, available, and valuable to your target audience. When you act on this regularly, you provide fuel to your fans, which in turn ignites others to join your brand community. You are well on your way to becoming a revered brand. But perhaps you're feeling a little overwhelmed, or you're asking yourself, "How could I possibly make all this happen?" Not to worry. In chapter 12, I'll share with you a technique for turning one activity into a full year's worth of digital branding. I'll also show you how to move yourself outside the normal hierarchy at your company by becoming a digital brand ambassador.

CHAPTER 12

Lead the Way

For Your Community, Colleagues, and Company

Well, you've made it all the way to chapter 12. Bravo!

I'm thinking you might be feeling a bit accomplished and inspired . . . and perhaps a little overwhelmed. My clients tell me that they understand why it's important to craft compelling messages and be active with social media, they see the connection to career success, and they're excited about flexing their digital brand muscle. Then they say:

"I already have a full-time job. How can I possibly do all this without feeling stressed and overworked?"

If you can relate to that question, good. In this chapter, I'll share ways to maximize the impact of a small number of activities to ensure that your target audience perceives you as visible, available, and valuable without making you feel vanquished. It's not just about being efficient; it's about recognizing the return on investment.

I'll show you how you can use your new social savvy to drive greater value for your colleagues and your company while increasing your impact and internal brand value. But the rewards become exponential when you become a true digital branding leader, inspiring others in your professional community to unearth and celebrate their own unique personal brands. Brands that are rooted in imitation or illusion are exhausting to maintain, and it's a struggle (sometimes an impossible one) to make them fruitful. But brands that are rooted in authenticity flourish easily; a little TLC goes a long way.

So what exactly does that TLC entail? How do you accomplish all this digital brand building without adding stress to your life?

Find Your Path to Selective Fame

As long as you took the time to identify your true self in the early chapters of this book, the secret lies in simply combining these three techniques:

- **Maximizing.** Make the most of every opportunity. Create less while increasing the impact of everything you craft.
- **Linking.** Connect real- and virtual-world communications activities. Too many professionals believe their real-world personal branding activities are unrelated to digital branding. This mindset is not only extremely inefficient; it can also lead to mixed messages about your brand. To maximize the value of your personal branding efforts, your real-world activities should be synced with your social media actions. This creates powerful synergies that amplify your message for an audience of millions.
- **Focusing.** Focus your time more on promotion than creation. Use the 80/20 rule. Spend 20 percent of the time creating your content and 80 percent of the time making that content visible to all the right people.

The most productive path to selective fame requires that you think of yourself as a thought leader and commit to sharing your knowledge, expertise, and opinions with your stakeholders. Content creation is often the biggest stressor for those who want to grow their brand through thought leadership. Even the most ambitious digital branders can feel inundated when it comes to increasing visibility with their target audience.

In addition to maximizing, linking, and focusing, there's one other tactic that not only saves time but also helps you distill your brand essence. It's my favorite personal branding technique, and it's guaranteed to help lighten the load.

Committing to one. Identify just one brand-building activity each year. Then turn it into a year's worth of digital branding by applying the three techniques described.

Before you start, identify one brand-building activity to pursue this year. For this example, I'll use the goal of delivering one thought-leadership presentation to your local professional association. The process that I outline will help you build an entire year's worth of digital branding from this one activity. The goal is for this to excite and energize you rather than exhaust or exasperate you. The key is to plan in advance and schedule activities throughout the year.

Here are the three steps of the process (Figure 12-1).

Figure 12-1. The 3 Ps of Visibility

1. Prepare

Create the speaking opportunity.

Choose the organization. Research relevant professional associations that host regular meetings that include a speaker (or internal opportunities if that makes more sense for you). Prioritize the ones that give you the best brand-building platform (your people are in the audience, their events are professional and well attended). Choose the organization that could truly benefit from your expertise.

Choose your topic. To make this activity deliver maximum value, choose a topic that sits at the intersection of these three brand-builders:

- It helps you expand your thought leadership and express your point of view.
- It is relevant to your target audience (the people who are making decisions about you).
- It has a long shelf-life (it's not tied to current events).

Secure your gig. Offer to speak, and choose a time and date for your presentation. It's OK if it will take place far in the future. That'll give you more time to prepare. Remember: When you're planning your speech, arrange with the organizer to have your speech recorded on video. If they don't or won't do this, make your own arrangements for video recording.

Engage your network. Ask members of your network through Twitter and LinkedIn what they would like to see in the presentation. What are their hot buttons related to your topic?

Research Twitter and LinkedIn groups for content to include in your presentation, and reach out to the creators of that content asking for permission to reference their work—further building your network.

Build your presentation. Create the presentation with a combination of words and images (apply what you learned in chapter 7 about your PBID). Make sure you use all the SEO keywords relevant to your area of thought leadership multiple times throughout the slides. Include as many of these items as appropriate:

- Images that reinforce your key points—use the image resources we identified in chapter 8.
- Quotes from people in your brand community (your boss, colleagues, and so on). Remember to include quotes from respected thought leaders in your field as well.

- Quotes from famous people.
- Catchphrases that you are (or want to be) known for. Martha Stewart is known for saying "It's a good thing." Tim Gunn says "Make it work." Matthew McConaughey is known for saying "Alright, alright, alright." If you have one, include it. If you don't, don't create one. Be your natural self, not a manufactured tagline.
- Questions for the audience (for informal polls): "How many of you have ever googled yourself?" Or, "Who here works for a company that uses X client-management software?" Remember to comment on those numbers after the audience responds, and keep track of those numbers. It's anecdotal but useful data.
- A unique hashtag for tweeting about your content.
- Three to five key messages that are important to your brand, capturing how you want to be known.
- A thank-you slide at the end showing not only your contact info but also the ways you would like to add the audience to your brand community. For example, you could include a link to your LinkedIn profile.

Publicize the event. Tweet about your presentation. Once the event is up on the association's website, tweet a link to it, inviting your followers to attend. Even if they don't attend, you're letting people know you're a sought-after speaker. Do the same with your LinkedIn activity feed and relevant LinkedIn groups.

Tweet and update your LinkedIn activity feed just before you are leaving for the event, letting your followers know you are about to deliver a presentation. Express your enthusiasm for the topic.

Pull it all together. Name the presentation you create with both your name and the relevant keywords you want to be known for. If you don't already have them, create social media accounts in LinkedIn, Twitter, SlideShare, Instagram, and YouTube (substitute your favorite social media platforms as appropriate). Then, get the message out about your upcoming presentation. Use your social media and email list to let your target audience know about your upcoming talk. And arrange to have a friend or colleague there who can help you make the most of this presentation. Before you leave to deliver your presentation, alert your brand community with a tweet or a LinkedIn update, and include a link to the event description.

2. Present

Now, it's time to shine. Ask your friend or colleague you brought with you to take some photographs of you presenting.

Deliver the best presentation ever. During the presentation:

- Introduce your custom hashtag and encourage audience members to tweet and use other social media to share content with their audience, reminding them to use the hashtag in their communications. This will help make you visible to their brand communities. You can even have the hashtag appear on every slide as a reminder.
- Poll the audience with your prepared questions, letting them answer simply by raising their hand. Make a note of the responses for future reference. Don't count—just get a feel for audience response: "About a third of you raised your hand."
- Remind yourself you are being recorded so you can get clips to use later. When you share your key messages, speak directly to the camera so you can have those important elements recorded for future use.

Make it easy for the audience to contact you:

- Give them info. Leave a one-page handout with valuable content and resources, and include your contact information. Think about how you want them to connect with you—connect on LinkedIn, subscribe to your YouTube channel, follow you on Twitter. The handout can even include your LinkedIn QR code that they can scan to directly access your profile.

- Keep the conversation going. As I said in the "Build Your Presentation" checklist, end the presentation with a thank-you slide that includes your contact info, encouraging the audience to connect on LinkedIn or follow you on Twitter. This will help you grow your network.

3. Profit

With the presentations behind you, phew! You have the MS PowerPoint or Mac Keynote slides and the video file of your brilliant performance, along with the pics your friend snapped of you as you spoke and the raw video footage. That's all you need to create and share an entire year of social media content. Here's how to profit from all that preparation and expand your visibility from the 50 people who were in the room to 50,000 people or more.

SlideShare

Create a PDF of the presentation and post it to your SlideShare account. Remember to use the right keywords so it can be found when people are searching. The great thing about SlideShare is that it automatically creates a transcript of everything you typed into your presentation. It displays right below your PDF.

YouTube

Turn your presentation video into a series of clips. The clips should be:

- Valuable to your audience—offering helpful insights.
- Able to stand alone.
- One to three minutes long. Remember, attention spans are waning.

Add your video bumper to brand the videos (not to worry if you skipped that step in the PBID section of chapter 8, but now's the time to create a bumper if you haven't already). Then, upload them to your YouTube account as "Private" so you can release them throughout the year.

Instagram

Post the photos your friend took of you and the relevant images you included in your presentation to your Instagram account, adding all the right hashtags. You can also easily create images using the quotes from your presentation with tools like Canva. Add the quotes over your branded textures. Space out the posts over months or the entire year.

Twitter

Search for the unique hashtag you created. Then, retweet all tweets that were made during your presentation. And tweet what you learned from your audience polling. For example, write "About two-thirds of audience members said they believe investment will increase in robotics in their company," then include a link to the SlideShare presentation. Also, tweet all the quotes you included in your presentation (from famous people and industry thought leaders), including attributions. Remember to alert the thought leaders in your tweets to get on their radar.

Grow your brand community by following all the people who tweeted and thanking them for coming to your presentation. Just search on the custom hashtag you created—searchability is the real power of that tiny piece of punctuation.

LinkedIn

Share your thoughts in an update about what you learned in the presentation:

- Turn the transcript of the presentation (obtained from SlideShare) into a 600-1,000-word blog.
- Publish the blog and share an update with all your connections.
- Post a link to the blog to all relevant LinkedIn groups, with additional commentary.
- Post relevant video clips to the Summary and Experience sections of your LinkedIn profile.
- Reach out to the connections you quoted in the presentation, and give them the link so they can share it with their communities.

Sound exhausting? Actually, it's not. Creating the primary content for the presentation is the most intensive part of the process. The follow-up activities are spread throughout the year and don't require you to generate new concepts. You can actually accomplish all of this in just nine minutes a day if you commit to doing it daily. Just pen your nine minutes into your calendar or daily to-do list.

You can also use social media management tools like Buffer or Hootsuite to streamline and automate the process.

If you're muttering, "This sounds good, but I hate public speaking," know that you're not alone. Public speaking is listed ahead of death in many surveys about fears. Jerry Seinfeld famously quipped that at a funeral people would rather be in the coffin than delivering the eulogy. If you don't like public speaking, I suggest you work to get over the fear. There are so many resources to help, like Toastmasters (which helps you grow your network along the way). Being a good public speaker is guaranteed to have a positive impact on your career.

And if you just aren't ready to do that, no worries. Substitute your favorite communications medium and refine the process to fit that. For example, if you like long-form writing, produce a whitepaper. Then, break it up into a series of articles, and then tweet statistics and quotes from it.

If you apply this three-step process to just one highly polished real-world activity each year, you can turn it into an entire year's worth of personal branding exposure on the web with minimal effort, setting a great example of someone who makes an impact without depleting those limited resources of time and energy.

Become a Proactive Ambassador and a Digital Advocate

The "commit to one" technique will help you amp up your brand across all the elements of your brand community, primarily focusing on your external connections (although as we discussed in part 1, your internal colleagues will be using Google to learn about you, too).

To truly become a leader as part of your internal brand and demonstrate your social savvy, you need to become a digital brand ambassador for your company. Your organization needs you to demonstrate your digital dexterity. When you do, you show up as an innovative social savvy superstar. According to Dave Kerpen, chairman of Likeable Media, "Increasingly, we'll see the rise of the 'social company,' whether it's using LinkedIn to share company news with the world, or an increasing number of CEOs using Twitter to become chief evangelists" (Arruda 2017).

Yet, according to PwC, CEOs think their people are not digitally equipped. Seventy-six percent of CEOs are concerned about the lack of digital skills within their workforce. Bridging this gap is crucial because companies that engage all their people in their digital marketing strategy will outperform their competitors. Consider these statistics in four core elements of the business:

Sales:

- Employees with socially encouraging employers are significantly more likely to help boost sales than employees who don't have that support—72 percent versus 48 percent, according to the Australian communications firm Weber Shandwick.

- According to the social media branding company BRANDfog, 77 percent of buyers are more likely to buy from a company whose CEO uses social media.
- 78 percent of salespeople who use social media perform better than their peers.

Marketing:

- According to LinkedIn, employees have 10 times more connections than their company has followers.
- 79 percent of firms surveyed reported more online visibility after the implementation of a formal employee advocacy program; 65 percent reported increased brand recognition.
- Leads developed through employee social marketing convert seven times more frequently than other leads.

People—Recruiting and Retention:

- 80 percent of employees say they would rather work for a social CEO, according to a Weber Shandwick study.
- Employees of socially engaged companies are 20 percent more likely to stay at their company and 27 percent more likely to feel optimistic about their company's future.
- 98 percent of employees use at least one social media site for personal use; of them, 50 percent are already posting about their company.

Reputation/PR:

- Social CEOs are much more likely to be seen as good communicators, compared to unsocial CEOs (55 percent versus 38 percent, respectively).

- 84 percent of consumers value recommendations from friends and family above all forms of advertising—additionally, 77 percent of consumers are likely to make a purchase after hearing about it from someone they trust.

If you needed some motivation, that avalanche of statistics should help you get moving. When you take on the role of digital brand ambassador, you propel yourself outside the normal hierarchy and become open to and connected with more of the organization. You demonstrate your loyalty, expand your knowledge of what's happening outside your role, build your brand visibility, and stand out from your peers.

Dozens of tools, services, and platforms like Dynamic Signal, Influitive, AdvocateHub, Hootsuite Amplify, SocialHP, and Voicestorm are springing up to help companies engage their people in their digital strategy. Cheryl Burgess, CEO of Blue Focus Marketing and co-author of *The Social Employee*, puts it this way:

"Social employees are the preferred new marketing channel.
They are a bridge from the inside world to the outside and the most important
tool in your arsenal. Much like an octopus, social employees have eight times
the reach—but they're more trusted than branded channels and better equipped
to respond to customer needs quickly and effectively."

To be a digital brand steward, first decide on the scope of your role:

Solo (grape). If your company already has a program to engage their people, you'll commit to being a superstar proponent. Even if they don't, you can still have an impact.

Group (bunch of grapes). If you want to be the leader for your team, department, or division, you'll need to involve others. What you will build can be part of a corporate-wide initiative after you have proven the value.

Entire organization (vineyard). If you want to make a name for yourself throughout your company, becoming the person who spearheads this initiative would certainly help you stand out. If you work in talent development, marketing, or communications, this might be a natural fit.

Regardless of the scenario, when you commit to being a digital steward of the brand, you:

- Become more aware and involved in things that are happening throughout the company outside your role.
- Demonstrate your loyalty to your employer by amplifying their digital branding efforts.
- Get content you can use to build your brand while supporting the company brand.
- Showcase your skills outside your "day job."

And take it in small bits, not big bites. In other words, don't try to take on all social media platforms. It's why I emphasize starting with LinkedIn throughout this book. It's the:

- most professional of all social media
- least common denominator—the tool more of the people at your company use than any other
- gateway—opening the door to other social media.

Before embarking on any of these three digital steward scenarios, check out your company's social media policies. You don't want to be the leader in getting the message out and end up on the Untrustables list because you violated a company policy.

Now let's apply each of those scenarios with real action.

Be a Grape: Work Solo

If your company has a digital brand ambassador program and is using tools like Amplify or SocialHP, commit to becoming their most fervent leader.

To do that, share content your company creates that is relevant to your target audience.

✔ DO THIS,
✘ NOT THAT

Do add your point of view when sharing company content and any info that will make the content more valuable and more branded.	**Don't** just blindly share any content your company creates; don't share without adding your personal touch.

If your company does not have an official program for engaging employees, take it upon yourself to get involved. Follow your company's LinkedIn page (you're already following it if you clicked on the link when you added your company to the Experience section of your profile). Then regularly check your feed for content coming from your company. When there is content that's relevant to your target audience, share it, along with your thoughts. Remember to share it with all relevant groups beyond your connections. It will have a bigger impact.

Do this for all your company's communications channels where you would like to be present. Remember to include all hashtags.

Augment what comes from your communications people with your own messages about your company. You might include things like:

- So proud to be working for a company with a culture of learning. Today I attended an inspiring session about #leadership. @CompanyName
- Today, my employer @CompanyName announced a new commitment to diversity, acknowledging the value of differences in the workforce.
- Our CEO @CEOname offered this insightful quote about #customerservice during our all-hands meeting today.

- My company lets me work from home 3 days a week, which makes me so much more productive (and happier too!). Thanks @companyname #flex

When you get actively and consistently involved with your company's communications, you put yourself on the radar of people throughout the organization.

Be a Bunch of Grapes: Engage a Group

If you're the leader of a team or a member of a team and you're looking to make your mark, leading a social savvy initiative will help you engage the members in your team and create some new energy and thinking. As always, I recommend LinkedIn as the ideal starting point.

One great approach is to establish a friendly team competition. If you're the leader, this is how to make it happen. If you're not the leader, make this pitch:

- **Digital Dexterity.** Being digitally enabled is the key to success in the future. Everyone on the team will benefit from learning these skills.
- **Team Visibility.** When the team is fully engaged in a social savvy program, members will stand out individually, and the team itself will start to attract the positive attention of leaders and others throughout the organization.
- **Fun.** A team competition is an enjoyable way to unify team members, regardless of level and role, and get them thinking outside their daily to-do lists.

Then, build your team competition:

- **Establish the baseline.** Evaluate all the team profiles for both quantity (completeness) and quality (compellingness).

- **Set the goal.** Train others in the concepts you've mastered by reading this book:
  - Build a stellar LinkedIn profile.
  - Grow your network and join groups.
  - Become a digital brand ambassador.
- **Set the ground rules for the competition.**

Be a Vineyard: Tap the Entire Organization

If you're a super overachiever and want to take on a high-potential, major-impact project in your company, or you work in the fields of marketing, communications, talent development, or PR and already know that this is an element of your role, offer to build an organization-wide social media program. Few companies have tapped into the full potential of social media—delivering a huge advantage to those organizations that choose to develop company-wide social media programs. Here's the seven-step process:

1. Assemble the Team

As with most corporate initiatives, the program lives or dies by the people leading it. Get the right people involved. The right mix of disciplines, along with a high level of enthusiasm for the project (especially among influential leaders who are even respected by those outside their functional area), will go a long way toward building a successful program.

2. Establish a Baseline

Understand who in the organization currently has a profile. Evaluate the quality of the various profiles. Record how many followers you have on your company page. Do as much as you can to understand the current situation so you can measure the impact of the transformative work you're about to do.

3. Search for the Stars

There are likely people in your organization who are LinkedIn superstars, regularly engaging in conversations on the platform. Involve them in the process.

4. Set Goals

So you can see how much you are moving the needle, define your objectives.

 PONDER THIS

- What will make this program a success?
- What percentage of employees do you want using LinkedIn?
- How much increase do you want to achieve in social interactions of your company content?
- By what percentage do you want to increase your company page followers?

Aggregate the data so you have a company-wide picture of your starting point. Then make sure to track and measure your progress.

5. Start at the Top

Your people will look to the company's leaders as role models. Before rolling out the program, make sure your leaders all have stellar profiles and are using LinkedIn as a tool to stay connected to stakeholders. For key leaders, create a scorecard that includes measures for:

- profile completeness
- profile quality
- network connections and follower stats
- activity.

The scoring process shouldn't feel judgmental, and it might require a higher touch approach than you will be able to roll out to everyone. For anyone who needs help, share sample high-scoring profiles and case studies from your company's social savvy superstars.

6. Train Talent

With most of my clients, I find a three-stage LinkedIn talent development program works best:

- **Profiles.** This stage is about building a perfect LinkedIn profile that is authentic, compelling, and high quality. Your network won't work if your profile does not impress viewers. Your profile should make them want to get to know you.
- **People.** This stage has to do with connections and groups— building your network and understanding how to use LinkedIn as your contact management system.
- **Performance.** This final stage leads to doing your job better. Teach employees how to use LinkedIn to demonstrate their thought leadership, solve problems, source staff, nurture their network, and open doors to clients and partners.

To make your initiative more pervasive, integrate LinkedIn modules into all relevant talent development programs, from orientation to high-potential initiatives and executive coaching programs. For orientation, make sure to build a consistent LinkedIn session into your onboarding protocol, helping new hires get the basics. Include evidence that shows why LinkedIn is important and what your company provides in terms of support. Employees who are coming from a previous company that blocked LinkedIn will find your approach liberating—and they'll see the wisdom in blending their personal branding efforts with your corporate brand strategy.

Continuing education is crucial for a constantly evolving tool like LinkedIn. Train-the-trainer programs are especially helpful for encouraging teams to be more involved.

7. Evaluate and Elucidate

At appropriate intervals (quarterly is particularly appropriate for publicly traded companies), look at the progress you are making toward the measured goals you established at the outset of the program.

BRAND HACK

Use these best practices to ensure success:

- **Make it count.** Build this into your employees' objectives. When you tie the program to performance, employees will see how important it is to the organization.
- **Make it fun.** Amp up the fun factor by creating contests, featuring and highlighting profiles that are compelling, and starting a friendly competition among various departments.
- **Make it meld.** Link it to other initiatives, like your corporate intranet, which likely works a lot like LinkedIn. Rather than thinking of these as separate tools, you can let them do double duty by treating them as two connected and integrated tools. When employees write their bio for your intranet, have them use that as the starting point for their LinkedIn summary.
- **Make it connective.** Use it to connect employees with each other. Distribute the list of attendees at corporate events, particularly at training sessions. Have them download the LinkedIn app on their phones, enabling them to get connected in real time.

BRANDI BRAINSTORMS

I'm pumped! I'm going to commit to amp up the social media savvy at my company. We're a little bit like "the cobbler's children" here. Although we help our clients with social media, we're not engaging our own people in it.

I'm going to start with my team as a six-month beta program. I'll partner with HR, communications, and IT. Once I have data (have I told you that I love data?!), I'm going to create an infographic that explains what we did and the results we achieved. I'll use video to sell it to my manager and propose that we take on the project for the entire organization, globally. This project has all the things I love—creativity, challenge, collaboration— and so many opportunities to showcase my brand. I'm on it!

Summing Up

In this chapter, I shared a lot of counterintuitive advice. I told you to steal others' content and be lazy. I hope this unconventional technique made you chuckle . . . and will help you remember, and act on, the strategies I shared. To put those strategies into action and make sure the learning from this book is applied, I've provided some final pointers in the afterword that will help turn your "to do" into a "to done," and even an applause-worthy "ta-da." These are the keys to becoming a true leader in your community and your company. But before we get to that, I want to acknowledge you.

You impress me!

You made it all the way through this book and you're well on your way to being a socially savvy leader. You've probably felt uncomfortable or awkward at times. Maybe some of what I shared made you squirm. But you stuck with it and took away a series of actions along with ideas for new mindsets to adopt and habits to embrace. I'm confident you have what you need to be a brand in demand.

Afterword

That's it!

Your brand has moved online and your potential for a wildly successful and fulfilling career has moved with it. When you master digital branding, you'll be truly real in the virtual world. That will help you build a community of fervent fans and promoters who can help you reach your goals. In my self-appointed role of chief encouragement officer, I provide this final advice to reinforce the key themes woven into this book:

- **Be of value.** When your efforts are founded in supporting others, you'll make a powerful and positive impact.
- **Be involved.** Strong brands don't go it alone. Be an active member of relevant communities.
- **Be consistent.** Strong brands are known for something, not 100 things. Be clear and consistent with your message.
- **Be constant.** You don't need to become a digital branding machine. Just commit to taking action regularly. Strong brands don't go into hiding.
- **Be a lifelong learner.** Social media and everything in the online world is evolving rapidly. Stay on top of what's happening so you can demonstrate your digital fitness.

And above all, **be yourself.** Authenticity goes a long way in the real and virtual world. Have the courage to be yourself—your best self—and watch your career soar.

References

Introduction

Arruda, W. 2018. "How to Make Your Workplace Ready for Gen Z." *Forbes,* November 13. www.forbes.com/sites/williamarruda/2018/11/13/how-to-make-your-workplace-ready-for-gen-z/#1ee7e5134d30.

Arruda, W. 2017. "2017 Personal Branding Trends Part 3: The Rise of the Social Employee." *Forbes,* January 3.

Atkinson, J. 2018. Personal communication with author, September.

Awan, A. 2017. "The Power of LinkedIn's 500 Million Community." LinkedIn Official Blog, April 24. https://blog.linkedin.com/2017/april/24/the-power-of-linkedins-500-million-community.

Bank of America. 2018. "Trends in Consumer Mobility." https://promo.bankofamerica.com/mobilityreport/assets/images/BOA_2018-Trends-in-Consumer-Mobility-Report-FINAL-2.pdf.

Burgess, C., and M. Burgess. 2013. *The Social Employee: How Great Companies Make Social Media Work.* New York: McGraw-Hill Education.

Burgess, M. 2019. Personal email with author.

Burke, D. 2017. "Why Employee Advocacy Can't Wait." LinkedIn Marketing Solutions Blog, March 2. https://business.linkedin.com/marketing-solutions/blog/linkedin-elevate/2017/why-employee-advocacy-cant-wait.

Cisco. Nd. "VNI Forecast Highlights Tool." www.cisco.com/c/m/en_us /solutions/service-provider/vni-forecast-highlights.html.

Davies, D. 2018. "Meet the 7 Most Popular Search Engines in the World." *Search Engine Journal*, January 7. www.searchenginejournal .com/seo-101/meet-search-engines/#close.

Ellis, S. 2017. "How to Motivate Your Team on Thinking Like Entrepreneurs and not Employees." Hibox, December 1. www.hibox.co/blog/how-to -get-your-team-thinking-like-entrepreneurs-not-employees.

Graham, D. 2018. *Switchers: How Smart Professionals Change Careers and Seize Success.* New York: AMACOM.

Graham, D. 2018. Personal email with author, September 16.

Howington, J. 2018. "Survey Explores Varying Attitudes of Millennials and Older Workers about Key Workplace Issues." Flexjobs, September 17. www.flexjobs.com/blog/post/survey-finds-varying -attitudes-millennials-older-workers-about-key-workplace-issues.

Joel, M. 2013. *Ctrl Alt Delete: Reboot Your Business. Reboot Your Life. Your Future Depends on It.* New York: Hachette.

Jones, J.M. 2015. "In U.S., Telecommuting for Work Climbs to 37%." Gallup Poll Social Series, August 19. https://news.gallup.com/poll /184649/telecommuting-work-climbs.aspx.

Lidsky, D. 2005. "Me Inc.: the Rethink." *Fast Company*, March 1. www.fastcompany.com/55257/me-inc-rethink.

Marker, S. 2015. "How Many Jobs Will the Average Person Have in His or Her Lifetime?" LinkedIn, February 22. www.linkedin.com/pulse /how-many-jobs-average-person-have-his-her-lifetime-scott-marker.

Mushroom Networks. Nd. "YouTube – The 2nd Largest Search Engine (Infographic)." www.mushroomnetworks.com/infographics/youtube ---the-2nd-largest-search-engine-infographic.

Palmer, K., and D. Blake. 2018. *The Expertise Economy: How the Smartest Companies Use Learning to Engage, Compete, and Succeed.* Boston: Nicholas Brealey.

Peters, T. 1997. "The Brand Called You." *Fast Company,* August 31. www.fastcompany.com/28905/brand-called-you.

Previte, J. 2019. "The 2019 Digest of the Most Valuable Company Culture Statistics." BluLeadz, February 11. www.bluleadz.com/blog/annual-digest-of-company-culture-statistics.

Reynolds, B. 2018. Personal email with author, November 28.

Ryan, C. 2018. "Computer and Internet Use in the United States: 2016." United States Census Bureau, Report Number ACS 39, August 8. www.census.gov/library/publications/2018/acs/acs-39.html.

Shove, G. 2013. "Marketing That Money Can't Buy—Getting Employees to Tweet About Work." *Fast Company,* November 22.

Tran, K. 2017. "Viewers Find Objectionable Content on YouTube Kids." *Business Insider,* November 7. www.businessinsider.com/viewers-find-objectionable-content-on-youtube-kids-2017-11?utm_source=feedly&utm_medium=referral.

U.S. Department of Labor. Bureau of Labor Statistics. 2017. "Number of Jobs, Labor Market Experience, and Earnings Growth Among Americans at 50: Results from a Longitudinal Study." News Release, August 24. www.bls.gov/news.release/pdf/nlsoy.pdf.

Weber, B. 2013. "By the Year 2020, Almost Half of the Workforce Will Be Made Up of These People." Upworthy, September 9. www.upworthy.com/by-the-year-2020-almost-half-of-the-workforce-will-be-made-up-of-these-people-5.

Workplace Trends. 2018. "The Work Connectivity Study." News Release, November 13. https://workplacetrends.com/the-work-connectivity-study.

Chapter 1

Branson, R. 2018. "Discovering Original." Richard Branson's Blog, April 9. www.virgin.com/richard-branson/discovering-original.

Cain, S. 2019. Podcast Interview, Happier with Gretchen Rubin, February.

Olivet Nazarene University. 2018. "Study Explores Professional Mentor-Mentee Relationships in 2019." June. https://online.olivet.edu /research-statistics-on-professional-mentors.

Chapter 3

Solomon, L. 2015. "The Top Complaints From Employees About Their Leaders." *Harvard Business Review,* June 24. https://hbr.org/2015/06 /the-top-complaints-from-employees-about-their-leaders.

Tawakol, O. 2018. "I'm a CEO and the Most Underrated Business Skill Is One Most People Are Terrible At." *Business Insider,* August 16. www.businessinsider.com/communication-business-skill-2018-5.

Tschabitscher, H. 2019. "The Number of Emails Sent Per Day in 2019 (and 20+ Other Email Facts)." Lifewire, January 3. www.lifewire.com /how-many-emails-are-sent-every-day-1171210.

Chapter 4

Arruda, W. 2007. *Career Distinction: Stand Out by Building Your Brand.* Hoboken, NJ: Wiley.

Fontein, D. 2016. "The Ultimate List of LinkedIn Statistics That Matter to Your Business." Hootsuite Blog, November 22. https://blog.hootsuite .com/linkedin-statistics-business.

Haedrich, M. 1972. *Coco Chanel: Her Life, Her Secrets.* Boston: Little, Brown.

Gallant, J. 2019. "48 Eye-Opening LinkedIn Statistics for B2B Marketers in 2019." Foundation, January 1. https://foundationinc.co/lab/b2b -marketing-linkedin-stats.

Joel, M. 2013. *Ctrl Alt Delete: Reboot Your Business. Reboot Your Life. Your Future Depends on It.* New York: Hachette.

LinkedIn. Nd. "A Brief History of LinkedIn." https://ourstory.linkedin.com.

Omnicore. 2019. "LinkedIn by the Numbers: Stats, Demographics & Fun Facts. Blog, January 6. www.omnicoreagency.com/linkedin-statistics.

ROI Research. Nd. "About Us." https://researchoninvestment.com/company/about-us/.

Sanders, T. 2005. *The Likeability Factor: How to Boost Your L-Factor and Achieve Your Life's Dreams.* New York: Crown.

Yuan, L. 2018. "A Generation Grows Up in China Without Google, Facebook or Twitter." *New York Times,* August 6. www.nytimes.com/2018/08/06/technology/china-generation-blocked-internet.html.

Chapter 5

Ye, L. 2015. "27 Tweetable Quotes From Sales Rockstars Going to #INBOUND 15" (Jill Rowley). Hubspot, August 18. https://blog.hubspot.com/sales/tweetable-quotes-from-sales-rockstars-going-to-inbound15.

Chapter 6

Grandey, A.A., G.M. Fisk, A.S. Mattila, K.J. Jansen, and L.A. Sideman. 2005. "Is 'Service with a Smile' Enough? Authenticity of Positive Displays During Service Encounters." *Organizational Behavior and Human Decision Processes* 96:38-55.

Patel, S. 2017. "How Your Brand Can Capitalize on LinkedIn's New 'Lead Gen' Opportunities." *Entrepreneur,* June 19. www.entrepreneur.com/article/294649.

Savitz, E. 2011. "The Untapped Power of Smiling." *Forbes,* March 22.

TED. 2011. "Ron Gutman: The Hidden Power of Smiling." TED2011, March. www.ted.com/talks/ron_gutman_the_hidden_power_of _smiling?language=en.

Turner, M.L. 2017. "8 Ways to Get More LinkedIn Profile Views." Forbes, February 28.

Chapter 7

Arruda, W. 2018. "The Best LinkedIn Headshots and How to Create Yours." *Forbes,* September 5. www.forbes.com/sites/williamarruda /2018/09/05/the-best-linkedin-headshots-and-how-to-create-yours /#74bf6eb36d2f.

Callahan, S. 2018. "Picture Perfect: Make a Great First Impression with Your LinkedIn Profile Photo." LinkedIn Sales Blog, December 28. https:// business.linkedin.com/en-uk/marketing-solutions/blog/posts/content -marketing/2017/17-steps-to-a-better-LinkedIn-profile-in-2017.

Cournoyer, B. 2012. "21 Quotes on Why Video Marketing ROCKS." Brainshark.com, April 2. www.brainshark.com/ideas-blog/2012 /April/21-quotes-on-video-marketing.

Demand Gen Report. 2014. "The Power of Visual Content [Infographic]." September 17. www.demandgenreport.com/industry -topics/rich-media/2906-the-power-of-visual-content-infographic.

Hubspot. 2018. "The Ultimate List of Marketing Statistics for 2018." www.hubspot.com/marketing-statistics.

Instagram. Nd. "Instagram Business." https://business.instagram.com.

JDP. 2018. "Tips for Job Seekers." JDP Blog, August 7. www.jdp.com /blog/2018/08/07/linkedin-photos-research.

Jones, C. 2017. "Should You Smile on Your LinkedIn Profile?" Quora, May 26. www.quora.com/Should-you-smile-on-your-LinkedIn-profile.

Medina, J. 2014. *Brain Rules: 12 Principles for Surviving and Thriving at Work, Home, and School.* Seattle: Pear Press.

Nielsen, J. 2010. "Photos as Web Content." November 1. www.nngroup
.com/articles/photos-as-web-content.

Levie, W.H., and R. Lentz. 1982. "Effects of Text Illustrations: A Review
of Research." *Educational Communication and Technology: A Journal of
Theory, Research, and Development*, 30(4): 195-232.

Patrick, W. 2017. "Why You Should Smile in Your Online Photo."
Psychology Today, November 1. www.psychologytoday.com/us/blog/why
-bad-looks-good/201711/why-you-should-smile-in-your-online-photo.

Chapter 8

"216 Web Safe Colors List." https://websafecolors.info/color-chart.

Alter, A. 2013. *Drunk Tank Pink: And Other Unexpected Forces That Shape
How We Think, Feel, and Behave.* New York: Penguin.

Arruda, William. 2009. "Personal Branding Guru, William Arruda."
Video, May 5. www.youtube.com/watch?v=6paItEm2AF4.

Chris. 2012. "The 'Ritual of Unpacking' Your Brand." Riley Life Blog,
November 12. www.rileylife.com/blog/the-ritual-of-unpacking-your
-brand.

Easy Calculation.com. Nd. "Pantone to Hex Converter." www.
easycalculation.com/colorconverter/pantone-to-hex.php.

Edison Research. 2018. "The Podcast Consumer 2018." www.slideshare
.net/webby2001/the-podcast-consumer-2018.

Fishman, E. 2016. "How Long Should Your Next Video Be?" Wistia.com,
July 5. wistia.com/learn/marketing/optimal-video-length.

Hubspot. 2018. "The Ultimate List of Marketing Statistics for 2018."
www.hubspot.com/marketing-statistics.

Moo.com. 2018. "What Fonts Reveal About You: Type Tasting."
Interviews, May 8.

"Pantone Colours." www.pantone-colours.com.

Chapter 9

American Psychological Association. 2006. "Multitasking: Switching Costs." www.apa.org/research/action/multitask.

An, M. 2018. "The Future of Content Marketing: How People Are Changing the Way They Read, Interact, and Engage With Content." Hubspot Research. https://blog.hubspot.com/news-trends/the-future -of-content-marketing?_ga=2.200265006.1820862119.1553695687 -2066569307.1549998052.

Ayres, M., and J. Wellin. 2017. "How to Use Wistia: A Step-by-Step Guide." Hubspot Blog, March 14. https://blog.hubspot.com/marketing /how-to-use-wistia.

Bowman, M. 2017. "Video Marketing: The Future of Content Marketing." *Forbes*, February 3.

Bunting, J. 2018. "Ready to Get Started With Video Ads on LinkedIn? Here Are 9 Things You Need to Know." LinkedIn Sales and Marketing Solutions EMEA Blog, June 7. https://business.linkedin .com/en-uk/marketing-solutions/blog/posts/B2B-video/2018/Ready -to-get-started-with-video-ads-on-LinkedIn-Here-are-9-things-you -need-to-know.

Business Insider Intelligence. 2017. "Video Will Account for an Overwhelming Majority of Internet Traffic by 2021." *Business Insider*, June 12.

Cisco. 2019. "Cisco Visual Networking Index: Forecast and Trends 2017-2022." Whitepaper. www.cisco.com/c/en/us/solutions/collateral/service- provider/visual-networking-index-vni/white-paper-c11-741490.html.

Content Marketing Institute. 2016. "B2B Content Marketing: 2016 Benchmarks, Budgets, and Trends—North America." https://contentmarketinginstitute.com/wp-content/uploads /2015/09/2016_B2B_Report_Final.pdf.

Doeing, D. 2019. "58 Powerful Video Marketing Statistics for 2019."
https://learn.g2crowd.com/video-marketing-statistics.

Gupta, S. 2016. "Your Brain on Multitasking." CNN Health, August 1.
www.cnn.com/2015/04/09/health/your-brain-multitasking/index.html.

Heine, C. 2017. "In Four Years, YouTube Has Gone From a Million Hours
of Video Viewed to a Billion." *Adweek,* February 27. www.adweek.com
/digital/in-4-years-youtube-has-gone-from-100-million-hours-of-video
-viewed-a-day-to-1-billion.

Hubspot. 2018. "The Ultimate List of Marketing Statistics for 2018."
www.hubspot.com/marketing-statistics.

Just, M.A., T.A. Keller, and J. Cynkar. 2008. "A Decrease in Brain
Activation with Driving When Listening to Someone Speak." *Brain
Research,* 1205, April 18, 70-80. https://www.ncbi.nlm.nih.gov/pmc/
articles/PMC2713933/.

Mansfield, M. 2019. "27 Video Marketing Statistics That Will Have
You Hitting the Record Button." *Small Business Trends,* January 16.
https://smallbiztrends.com/2016/10/video-marketing-statistics.html.

McQuivey, J. 2008. "How Video Will Take Over the World." *Forrester
Report,* June 17. https://www.forrester.com/report/How+Video+Will+
Take+Over+The+World/-/E-RES44199#.

Patel, S. 2016. "85 Percent of Facebook Video Is Watched Without
Sound." Digiday, May 17. https://digiday.com/media/silent-world-
facebook-video/.

Polycom. 2017. "Global Survey of 24,000+ Workers Unearths the 'Need'
for Flexibility in Order for Businesses to Thrive." Press Release,
March 20. https://www.polycom.com/company/news/press-
releases/2017/20170321.html.

Sharp, E. 2014. "The First Page of Google's Search Results Is the Holy
Grail for Marketers." Protofuse Blog, April 30. https://www.protofuse.
com/blog/details/first-page-of-google-by-the-numbers/.

Stafford, L. 2017. "How to Incorporate Video into Your Social Media Strategy." *Forbes,* July 13. https://www.forbes.com/sites/yec/2017/07/13/how-to-incorporate-video-into-your-social-media-strategy/#40e6d07f7f2e.

Chapter 10

Baer. D. 2013. "Why You Need a Diverse Network." *Fast Company,* August 13. https://www.fastcompany.com/3015552/why-you-need-a-diverse-network.

Basler, R. ed. 1953. *The Collected Works of Abraham Lincoln.* 9 vols. New Brunswick, New Jersey: Rutgers University Press.

Epstein. D.M. 2009. *The Lincolns: Portrait of a Marriage.* New York: Ballantine Books.

Fang, Y., B. Francis, and I. Hasan. 2018. "Differences Make a Difference: Diversity in Social Learning and Value Creation." *Journal of Corporate Finance,* 48, February, 474-91. https://www.sciencedirect.com/science/article/pii/S0929119917306557.

Krawcheck, S. 2013. "My (New) Third Very Simple Rule of Networking." LinkedIn, August 5. https://www.linkedin.com/pulse/20130805103249-174077701-my-new-third-very-simple-rule-of-networking/.

Misner, I. 2004. "The Importance of Diversity in Networking." *Entrepreneur,* January 26. https://www.entrepreneur.com/article/68840.

Simmons, M. 2015. "The No. 1 Predictor of Career Success According to Network Science." *Forbes,* January 15. https://www.forbes.com/sites/michaelsimmons/2015/01/15/this-is-the-1-predictor-of-career-success-according-to-network-science/#64388d06e829.

Chapter 11

Arruda, W. 2017. "2017 Personal Branding Trends Part 3: The Rise of the Social Employee." *Forbes*, January 3. https://www.forbes.com/sites/williamarruda/2017/01/03/2017-personal-branding-trends-2017-part-3-the-rise-of-the-social-employee/#2b7007d784b8.

Bagadiya, J. 2019. "217 Social Media Marketing Statistics to Prep You for 2019." *Social Pilot*, January 3. https://www.socialpilot.co/blog/social-media-statistics.

Herrington, D. 2013. "10 Super Health Benefits of Strawberries." Care2 Healthy Living, July 24. https://www.care2.com/greenliving/10-super-health-benefits-of-strawberries.html.

Liedke, L. 2019. "100+ Internet Statistics and Facts for 2019." March 26. https://www.websitehostingrating.com/internet-statistics-facts/.

Marse, A. 2013. "9 Things You Can Learn About Copywriting From David Ogilvy." *Social Media Today*, May 12. https://www.socialmediatoday.com/content/9-things-you-can-learn-about-copywriting-david-ogilvy.

Stevens, J. 2018. "Internet Stats & Facts for 2019." Hosting Facts, December 17. https://hostingfacts.com/internet-facts-stats/.

Chapter 12

"Under the Influence: Consumer Trust in Advertising." 2013. Nielsen Newswire, September 17. https://www.nielsen.com/us/en/insights/news/2013/under-the-influence-consumer-trust-in-advertising.html.

Arruda, W. 2017. "2017 Personal Branding Trends Part 3: The Rise of the Social Employee." *Forbes*, January 3.

Brudner, E. 2015. "15 Social Selling Stats That Will Inspire You to Take Action." Hubspot, May 6; updated July 28, 2017.

Burgess, C., and M. Burgess. 2013. *The Social Employee: How Great Companies Make Social Media Work.* New York: McGraw-Hill Education.

eMarketer. 2012. "CEOs Who Tweet Held in High Regard." March 27. https://www.emarketer.com/Article/CEOs-Who-Tweet-Held-High-Regard/1008929.

Find and Convert. 2017. "Social Networking Tools for B2B Social Media Platforms." http://www.findandconvert.com/b2b-digital-marketing-services/marketing/technology/social-selling-tools.

Gallant, J. 2019. "48 Eye-Opening LinkedIn Statistics for B2B Marketers in 2019." Foundation, January 1. https://foundationinc.co/lab/b2b-marketing-linkedin-stats/.

Hinge Research Institute. Understanding Employee Advocacy on Social Media. https://hingemarketing.com/uploads/hinge-research-employee-advocacy.pdf.

ING. 2014. "2014 Study Impact of Social Media on News: More Crowd-Checking, Less Fact-Checking." https://www.ing.com/Newsroom/All-news/NW/2014-Study-impact-of-Social-Media-on-News-more-crowdchecking-less-factchecking.htm.

Marketing Advisory Network, The. 2017. *2017: Employee Advocacy Impact Study.* https://marketingadvisorynetwork.com/2017/07/17/2017-employee-advocacy-impact-study/.

PricewaterhouseCoopers. 2018. *PwC's 21st Survey: Talent.* https://www.pwc.com/gx/en/ceo-survey/2018/deep-dives/pwc-ceo-survey-talent.pdf.

Reply. "101 Social Selling Stats You Need to Know." https://reply.io/101-social-selling-stats.

Roth, D. 2015. "Why Vocal Employees Are a Company's Best PR." *Fast Company,* March 25. https://www.fastcompany.com/3044156/why-vocal-employees-are-a-companys-best-pr.

Solis, B. 2014. "Relationship Economics: How Social Is Transforming the World of Work." LinkedIn, July 10. https://www.linkedin.com/pulse/20140710161411-2293140-relationship-economics-how-social-is-transforming-the-world-of-work-infographic/.

Weber Shandwick. "Employee Activists Spark Movement in Digital Age." http://webershandwick.com.au/employee-activists-spark-a-new-social-movement-in-the-digital-age/.

About the Author

William Arruda is a motivational speaker, bestselling author, and a leading authority on the topic of personal branding. He has been at the forefront of the field since its inception, teaching everyone from interns to senior executives how to harness the power of authentic personal branding. He is the CEO (Chief Encouragement Officer) of Reach—the global leader in personal branding—and the co-founder of CareerBlast.TV—a personal and digital branding video learning platform for innovative companies. He regularly shares his thoughts on workplace trends and branding in his *Forbes* column. When he's not traveling to deliver keynotes, he splits his time between New York City and Miami Beach.

Index